How to Bypass Your Bypass

What Your Doctor Doesn't Tell You About Cholesterol and Your Diet

How to Bypass Your Bypass

What Your Doctor Doesn't Tell You About Cholesterol and Your Diet

Richard M. Fleming,
M.D., F.I.C.A., F.A.C.A.

Rutledge Books, Inc.   Bethel, CT

Rutledge Books, Inc.
8 F.J. Clarke Circle, Bethel, CT 06801

Manufactured in the United States of America

Cataloging in Publication Data
Fleming, Richard M.
  How to bypass your bypass: what your doctor
doesn't tell you about cholesterol and your diet /
Richard M. Fleming.
    p. cm.
  ISBN 1-887750-55-X
  1. Coronary heart disease—Prevention—Popular
works. 2. Cholesterol—Popular works. 3.
Hypercholesteremia—Prevention—Popular works.
4. Low cholesterol diet—Recipes. I. Title.

616.12305--dc21   97-65228
                                      CIP

TABLE OF CONTENTS

Dedication

This book is dedicated to my wife and children without whose support and encouragement I could not have written it. They have endured countless hours of my being away from home, investigating heart disease, and writing this book. They have also helped develop and test many of the recipes which appear in this book. I would also like to thank my patients and friends who have shown how successfully people can reduce their cholesterol and weight with changes in their diet and lifestyles.

Genesis 1:29-30
Then God said, "I give you every seed-bearing plant on the face of the whole earth and every tree that has fruit with seed in it. They will be yours for food. And to all the beasts of the earth and all the birds of the air and all the creatures that move on the ground—everything that has the breath of life in it—I give every green plant for food." And it was so.

Daniel 1:5-17
The king assigned them a daily amount of food and wine from the king's table. They were to be trained for three years, and after that they were to enter the king's service. Among these were some from Judah: Daniel, Hananiah, Mishael, and Azariah. The chief official gave them new names: to Daniel, the name Belteshazzar; to Mishael, Meshach; and to Azariah, Abednego. But Daniel resolved not to defile himself with the royal food and wine, and he asked the chief official for permission not to defile himself this way. Now God had caused the official to show favor and sympathy to Daniel, but the official told Daniel, "I am afraid

of my lord the king, who has assigned your food and drink. Why should he see you looking worse than the other young men your age? The king would then have my head because of you." Daniel then said to the guard whom the chief official had appointed over Daniel, Hananiah, Mishael, and Azariah, "Please test your servants for ten days: Give us nothing but vegetables to eat and water to drink. Then compare our appearance with that of the young men who eat the royal food, and treat your servants in accordance with what you see." So he agreed to this and tested them for ten days. At the end of the ten days they looked healthier and better nourished than any of the young men who ate the royal food. So the guard took away their choice food and the wine they were to drink and gave them vegetables instead. To these four young men God gave knowledge and understanding of all kinds of literature and learning. And Daniel could understand visions and dreams of all kinds.

Introduction

Cholesterol has been considered a risk factor for coronary artery disease since the early 1900s. However, interest in investigating the role of dietary cholesterol and its relationship to coronary artery disease waited for the most part until the late 1960s. Many animals have shown cholesterol deposits in their arteries (atherosclerosis) when eating diets high in fat and cholesterol. It has also been shown that this process is reversible when the animals eat diets low in fat and cholesterol. We know that the same is true for people when we look at how much fat and cholesterol different groups of people eat and compare this with how much coronary artery disease they have. By the 1970s this type of epidemiologic information resulted in many studies which looked at how cholesterol could be reduced by medications. Some of the medications have since been removed from the market due to their potential side effects. Other medications are used today which have fewer potential problems than earlier drugs. However, people taking medications to help control their cholesterol and triglyceride levels still need to be monitored for possible adverse side effects.

In 1988 I was asked to join the Physician Cholesterol Education Faculty for the Iowa Heart Association. At that time 48% of the American people were dying from heart disease, primarily due to fat (atherosclerosis) build up in the arteries of their hearts. An average blood cholesterol at that time (little difference exists today) was 248 milligrams per deciliter (mg/dl), with the daily intake of fat exceeding 40% of the total calories consumed in a day. People were also eating an average of 500 milligrams (mg) of cholesterol daily. Despite beliefs that we have been changing our diets to reduce our risk of heart disease, little change has occurred since then. Part of the reason for this is probably because patient and physician attitudes have not really changed. There has been little consistent information and there is the every prevalent opinion that "it always happens to someone else and will never happen to me."

Many people can remember friends or relatives, 80 to 90 years old, who ate all the "bad" types of foods and were never sick a day in their life. But let's be totally honest with ourselves; our lives and the lives of our ancestors are considerably different. To begin with, their diets had less fat than ours do. At the beginning of the 20th century Americans ate approximately 1,000 more calories a day, but only 30% of those calories were from fat. They also worked longer hours with more strenuous labor, thereby using more calories, leaving less fat and cholesterol available for deposit in the arteries of their heart and elsewhere. There's one more important thing to remember—most of the people living in the early 1900s didn't live long enough to develop heart disease, or even cancer, because they died from something more deadly. Prior to the advent of Sir Alexander Fleming's discovery of penicillin, the number one cause of death was infectious diseases. You were the exception and not the rule if you lived long enough to develop cancer, heart disease, or any of a number of other health problems.

ALMOST 50 PERCENT OF ALL AMERICANS DIE FROM HEART DISEASE

We now know that for each 1% reduction in blood cholesterol there is a 2% reduction in your risk for developing atherosclerosis. Despite this understanding, the process of making changes in people's diets and lifestyles remains a problem. Many people are unwilling to make changes without consistent proof that it will help. Many others get mixed signals about whether they need to make changes in their diet or reduce their fat and cholesterol levels. Still, others who are willing to make changes lack the information necessary to help them make such changes. Unlike the traditional treatment of disease, the preventive approach requires the interactions of many health care providers of which your doctor is one member. He or she should always be included when making changes in your diet, lifestyles, and medications.

Recent studies (some of which I will share with you later in the book) have shown that fat and cholesterol levels can be significantly reduced in many individuals by diet alone. During the last three years research has shown the effect on cholesterol and triglyceride levels with changes in diet—with and without the use of medications. While many people suspected the outcome of such studies, I believe the results may surprise you. This book was designed to answer many of the questions people have regarding what types of changes they need to make in their diet if they want to reduce their weight, fat (triglyceride), and cholesterol levels. More importantly, it not only talks about the types of foods which are better for you, but gives you some ideas on how to prepare heart-healthy meals.

Where Does Cholesterol Come from and Where Does It Go?

There is more than one type of cholesterol which is used by your body for making the outer walls (membranes) of the cells of your body, steroid hormones (male and female sex hormones, etc.), and bile acids (gallbladder) necessary to digest fatty foods. Total cholesterol (TC) is made up of very low-density lipoprotein (VLDL) cholesterol, low-density lipoprotein (LDL) cholesterol, intermediate density lipoprotein (IDL) cholesterol, high-density lipoprotein (HDL) cholesterol, and chylomicrons as shown in the equation below. Additionally, there are three subtypes of HDL, designated as nascent HDL, HDL-2, and HDL-3. Also important are the triglycerides (TG), which represent "fat" and primarily appear as VLDL and chylomicrons.

$$TC = HDL + LDL + VLDL/5 + Chylomicrons + IDL$$

Because there is more than one type of cholesterol, there is more than one type of hyperlipidemia (high cholesterol and/or triglycerides) as shown in table one below. Depending upon which of these you may or may not have, different health problems can occur. As you can see from the table, more than 90% of all people with "hyperlipidemia" have either elevated LDL cholesterol and/or elevated triglycerides (VLDL) which are made by the liver and are related to the types of foods we eat.

Table One The six major types of hyperlipidemia.

Type	Elevated Lipoprotein	Elevated Lipid	Percent of US Population with Problem
I	Chylomicrons	TG*	<1
IIA	LDL	Chol**	10
IIB	LDL & VLDL	TG & Chol	40
III	IDL	TG & Chol	<1
IV	VLDL	TG	45
V	Chylomicrons & VLDL	TG	5

*TG is triglycerides, **Chol is cholesterol

THERE IS MORE THAN ONE TYPE OF CHOLESTEROL

Each of the various forms of cholesterol present in our bodies are either made in different areas of the body or consumed in our diet. Because cholesterol and fats are not water (blood) soluble they can only be carried through the bloodstream and recognized by the body if they are attached to proteins. Certain proteins are associated with the different types of cholesterol as shown in table two below. As you can see, each type of "cholesterol" is made up of differing percentages of cholesterol, triglycerides (fats), and proteins (apolipoprotein), as well as other minor components not shown here. This means that there is no such thing as either pure cholesterol or triglycerides, but rather combinations of the two which yield the different types of cholesterol. The relationship of these different types of cholesterol are shown in figure one.

Table Two The different types of cholesterol found in the body.

Type	Apolipoprotein*	%Cholesterol	%Triglyceride	%Protein
VLDL	E, C, B-100	20	55	7
LDL	B-100	55	5	20
IDL	E, B-100	40	25	20
HDL-2	A-I (liver) A-II (intestines)	25	5	40
HDL-3	A-I (liver) A-II (intestines)	20	5	55
Chylomicron	E, C, B-48, A	5	90	2

*Apolipoprotein "A" consists of A-I, A-II, and A-IV.
*Apolipoprotein "C" consists of C-I, C-II, and C-III.

CHOLESTEROL COMES FROM OUR DIET OR IS MADE BY OUR LIVER

Figure One Simplified version of the interactions between different types of cholesterol.

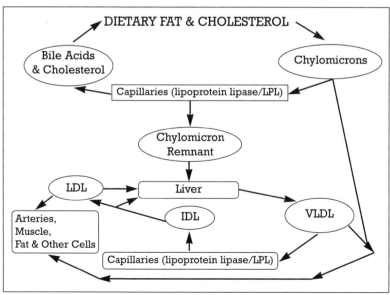

When foods which contain cholesterol and triglycerides (fats) are eaten and digested, they initially appear in the blood as chylomicrons, which resemble milk droplets. These chylomicrons represent approximately 98% of our dietary fat. Normally, chylomicrons remain in the blood from as little as a few minutes to as long as 12 to 14 hours. This is why correct measurements of the various types of cholesterol require 12 to 18 hours of fasting, which should allow sufficient time for the removal of chylomicrons from the blood.

In the smallest blood vessels (capillaries) present in our bodies, is an enzyme called lipoprotein lipase (LPL) which changes chylomicrons to chylomicron remnants. While this is occurring, HDL transfers cholesterol (cholesterol esters) to the chylomicron remnant, which takes the cholesterol to the liver for removal from the bloodstream. This is one of the ways in which "good" cholesterol (HDL) returns cholesterol to the liver, assuming the liver isn't already full. At the same time, free fatty acids (FFA) are released from the chylomicrons and are either stored as fat or delivered elsewhere throughout the body—for example muscles— where the FFA's supply energy for work. The chylomicron remnants are then taken up by the liver along with their cholesterol where it can be stored or made into VLDL cholesterol for release into the bloodstream.

HDL CHOLESTEROL IS A SCAVENGER

Recognizing that our teeth and jaws are more designed like those of herbivores than carnivores, our liver is extremely well designed for making cholesterol and triglycerides. The diet of herbivores consists mostly of fruits, grains, and vegetables. Smaller jaws with teeth designed for grinding these types of foods are found in people. This is in sharp contrast to carnivorous animals who have large fangs, no teeth for grinding, and large jaw muscles designed for biting and tearing flesh from their prey.

For herbivores to be able to make cholesterol for the needs of the body requires a liver that is able to take what little cholesterol is present in the diet, along with whatever excess calories are eaten, and make fats and cholesterol. This appears to be the characteristic of the human liver. Interestingly, such an efficiently designed liver will undoubtedly over manufacture cholesterol and fats if an abundance of cholesterol, fats, and calories are present in the diet. Like a factory, what comes out at the end of the production line is highly dependent upon what goes in. A typical American diet with 500 mg of cholesterol each day and more than 40% of the daily calories being fat calories, allows the liver to easily make 1,000 mg of cholesterol daily, which can then be deposited throughout our bodies.

As you can see from figure one, the liver gets its cholesterol from one of several sources, including the diet (chylomicron remnants), LDL, and HDL which transports cholesterol back to the liver from other areas of the body. In this manner, HDL serves as a scavenger, returning cholesterol to the liver. The scavenger mechanism of HDL appears to be important once the total cholesterol level exceeds 150 mg/dl, with a desired ratio of TC/HDL of 4.5 or less. The level of cholesterol necessary to make HDL an important factor undoubtedly varies from person to person. However, epidemiologic data suggests that in groups of people relatively free of coronary artery disease, the members have total cholesterol levels less than 150 mg/dl. These people also tend to have "low" HDL levels, suggesting that the overall level of cholesterol is not high enough to result in an increased risk of coronary artery disease despite "high" TC/HDL ratios. In other words, when total cholesterol levels are below 150 mg/dl, there does not appear to be an appreciable need for the scavenger mechanism of HDL cholesterol.

IF YOUR TOTAL CHOLESTEROL IS GREATER THAN 150MG/DL, IT IS IMPORTANT TO KEEP THE RATIO OF YOUR TOTAL CHOLESTEROL TO HDL LESS THAN 4.5

Once the liver gets cholesterol from the diet or the blood, it makes VLDL which is released back into the bloodstream. Like its chylomicron corollary, VLDL is changed by LPL (capillaries) to a "remnant" which is called intermediate density lipoprotein (IDL) cholesterol. As a result, FFAs are released for fat storage or muscle usage. Approximately half of the IDL is taken up by the liver while the other half becomes LDL cholesterol. It is the LDL cholesterol which carries approximately 75% of the cholesterol in our blood, making it available for deposit throughout the body. LDL cholesterol can circulate in the blood from minutes to hours until it is either deposited in the body (eg. the arteries of the heart) or returns to the liver where the whole process begins again. Although it may remain in the blood for as brief as a few minutes, LDL cholesterol can last for two to three days. Approximately half of the LDL will eventually be taken up by the liver, with the other half being deposited elsewhere.

While there appears to be more than one mechanism by which LDL can be taken up by the liver, the majority (~70%) occurs by a receptor known as B-100. Like a lock and key mechanism (figure two), the apolipoprotein B-100 (key) found with the LDL cholesterol (see table two above) fits into the receptor (lock) found on the liver. Occasionally some individuals have abnormal receptors (locks) or abnormal apolipoproteins (keys) resulting in problems where the LDL cholesterol cannot get into the liver, causing high LDL levels in the blood. These people are dependent upon the minor (30%) pathways for removal of LDL from the blood which are not as effective in removing cholesterol from the blood, resulting in higher LDL cholesterol levels than desirable. Once the liver is full of cholesterol, like the factory that has no more room to store raw materials, the doors to the liver (B-100 receptors) are closed resulting in a reduced uptake of LDL by the liver. Like the patient with an abnormal lock or key, there is an increase in LDL in the blood, leaving more of it available for deposit throughout the body, where it may not be needed.

Figure Two Lock and Key theory.

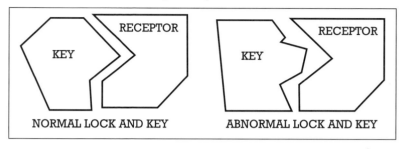

NORMAL LOCK AND KEY   ABNORMAL LOCK AND KEY

Depositing LDL in the arteries of the heart assures the heart of energy for emergency situations. For example, if you're on the plains of the Serengeti or in the mountains and you're being chased by lions and tigers and bears, it would be helpful to have a method for obtaining a lot of energy "fast." However, most of us are not involved with such life threatening scenarios. Today we tend to live more sedentary lifestyles. Subsequently, the deposit of cholesterol continues to accumulate over our lifetime until the arteries of our heart become too narrow to supply the necessary blood to keep us alive and a heart attack occurs. If we're lucky we get warning signs from our heart when we're too active, but in one-third to one-half of the people with heart disease, no warning signs occur until it's too late. For those who do survive, the injury to the heart cannot be reversed. Fortunately, we can survive heart attacks and live relatively normal lives depending upon where and how much of our heart is injured.

The deposit of LDL cholesterol in the arteries of our heart is further complicated by LDL's oxidation or the attachment of LDL to the walls of an artery. Once "oxidation" of LDL occurs it can be consumed by white blood cells called macrophages. The macrophage will later die and becomes a "foam cell." The "foam cell" is one of the hallmarks for atherosclerotic (coronary artery disease) heart disease. Antioxidant vitamins like beta-carotene, vitamin C and E appear to provide some protective effect by inhibiting the oxidation of LDL cholesterol.

7

How to Bypass Your Bypass

Certain health problems and medications can cause increases in cholesterol levels. When this happens, a person has a "secondary hyperlipidemia" because the increase in cholesterol is secondary (caused by) to something else. Reducing cholesterol levels in people with "secondary hyperlipidemias" depends upon treating the underlying problem, such as diabetes, alcohol consumption, steroid use, et cetera. Table three lists some of these problems and their effect upon VLDL (triglycerides), LDL, and HDL cholesterol.

PEOPLE SHOULD BE CHECKED FOR CAUSES OF SECONDARY HYPERLIPIDEMIA TO DETERMINE THE BEST POSSIBLE TREATMENT

Table Three Some causes of secondary hyperlipidemia.

Disease or Drug	VLDL	LDL	HDL
Alcohol	+	0	+
Anabolic Steroids	0	+	-
Androgens	0	+	-
Angiotensin Converting Enzyme Inhibitors	0	0	0
Beta-Blockers	+	0	-
Calcium Channel Blockers	0	0	0
Carbohydrate (High Sugar) Diets	+	+	-
Cyclosporine	0	+	0
Diabetes Mellitus	+	+	-
Diuretics (thiazide)	+	+	-
Estrogens	+	-	+
Glucocorticoids	+	+	0
Hypothyroidism	+	+	-
Nephrotic Syndrome	+	+	0

Disease or Drug	VLDL	LDL	HDL
Obesity	+	+	-
Pancreatitis	+	0	0
Polyunsaturated Fats	+	+	-
Pregnancy	+	+	+
Primary Biliary Cirrhosis	+	+	+
Weight Reduction	-	-	+

"+" means an increase, "0" means no significant change and "-" means a decrease

Both exercise and alcohol can increase HDL cholesterol levels. Remember however that HDL is simply a scavenger and doesn't actually remove cholesterol from the body, it simply moves it around. Significant increases in HDL do not appear to be possible with mild to moderate exercise or alcohol consumption alone. It is important to remember that excessive exercise or alcohol consumption is not without certain health risks. Excessive exercise can result in damage to joints, muscles, and other health problems. Well constructed exercise programs encourage stretching and aerobic (running, bicycling, swimming, etc.) conditioning followed by additional stretching, with the primary focus directed toward toning and strengthening your body.

Similarly, drinking alcohol may increase your HDL-3 level, but not sufficiently to produce any significant change in your TC/HDL ratio. It is also important to remember that alcohol has seven calories per gram (chapter three) which becomes fat if the calories are not used up. Too much alcohol, as shown in table three above, will lead to increases in your total cholesterol level by increasing your VLDL cholesterol. There are many other health problems related to drinking too much alcohol. The bottom line is that alcohol is not a drug treatment for high cholesterol.

ALCOHOL IS NOT A DRUG TREATMENT
FOR HIGH CHOLESTEROL

The overall impact of cholesterol and triglycerides on coronary artery (atherosclerosis) disease cannot be overstated. Currently, 48% of Americans and an even greater percentage of people in the UK, Scandinavian, and European countries die from heart disease. More than 500,000 Americans die yearly, with more than 1 million having heart attacks (myocardial infarction) and still millions more having chest pain (angina) from coronary artery disease. One third to one half of these people discover they have heart disease by dying from it.

It is estimated that 90% of the US population over the age of 30 have atherosclerotic lesions, primarily due to poor dietary habits. Autopsies on veterans from Korea and Vietnam demonstrated a significant amount of coronary artery disease in soldiers as young as 18 years of age. Despite the addition of new medications, new procedures, and surgery, the life span of patients with coronary artery disease is not significantly effected and it remains the number one killer of Americans. Interestingly enough, the only treatment which holds promise for the reduction of atherosclerosis is the control of risk factors for heart disease, of which cholesterol heads the list.

How Many Calories
Do You Need?

While eating can be a purely social event, the true purpose of eating is to provide the basic nutrients your body needs. These basic nutrients include proteins, carbohydrates, fats, vitamins, minerals, and water. The number of calories you need is determined by your current weight, activity level and overall health. For the purpose of this book we will assume that the reader is in good health. The challenge to successfully reducing your cholesterol and triglyceride levels is dependent upon reducing the amount of calories you eat in addition to reducing the cholesterol and fat in your diet. Many diets which restrict cholesterol (meats, cheeses, milk products, etc.) and fat consumption are somewhat liberal with regard to grains, cereals, pastas, et cetera; which can result in an overall increase in the number of calories eaten, causing an increase in weight, triglyceride levels, and eventually problems with increased cholesterol.

Regardless of the source of calories, excess calories are stored by the body. If the calories you eat exceed your needs then fat and cholesterol can be made by your liver. Presumably this will supply calories for a "rainy day" but more often than not these calories are permanently deposited and never used. Therefore if you are going to reduce your cholesterol and triglyceride (fat) levels, you must reduce these stores along with the number of calories you are eating. You must also watch what time of day you are eating. Calories eaten late in the day will probably not be used up by your body before going to sleep. This means that even if the number of calories you eat do not exceed the amount you need for the day—as far as your body is concerned—you ate more calories than you needed. While you sleep these excess calories can be turned into cholesterol and fat for a "rainy day."

In my practice I advise people not to eat after 7 P.M. assuming that they will go to sleep between 10 and 12 P.M. If the evening meal is one-third of your total (needed) calories for the day, then these calories should be used by your body either before you go to sleep or while you are sleeping. Not eating during the evening hours seems to be a problem for most Americans, leading to the term "couch potato." For the highly disciplined person this may not be a problem, for others, low calorie drinks like diet sodas, teas, or water, can provide substance without calories.

EATING LATE IN THE DAY MAY ENCOURAGE
YOUR LIVER TO MAKE FAT AND CHOLESTEROL
WHILE YOU SLEEP

Determining how many calories you need

The amount of calories you need is determined by your weight and activity level. A certain number of calories are needed each day to maintain your weight—this is called the basal metabolic (BMR) rate. Your BMR is 24 calories every day for every kilogram (kg) you weigh. Since there are 2.2 kg for every one pound you will need approximately **10 calories for each**

pound you weigh just to maintain your current weight.

10.9 calories per pound =

(24 calories/kg) (1 kg/2.2 lbs) =

(This may look complex, but it's actually pretty simple, especially if someone else does it for you.) To simplify further calculations we will use **10 calories per pound** of body weight to determine how many calories you need each day for your basal metabolic rate. Recent research has indicated that sudden changes in body weight by more than ten percent may adjust your BMR caloric needs. If this is the case, then reductions in weight beyond this may require decreasing your calorie intake to 8 calories per pound of body weight. As you might expect, increases in weight by more than ten percent appears to increase caloric needs, perhaps up to 12 calories per pound. Undoubtedly, further research will continue in this area while scientists attempt to better understand our bodies.

MOST PEOPLE NEED ABOUT 10 CALORIES A
DAY FOR EVERY POUND THEY WEIGH JUST
TO MAINTAIN THEIR CURRENT WEIGHT

While specific activities such as running, walking, bicycling, roller skating, washing dishes, etc. require a certain number of calories to perform, these are usually determined by your current weight and the amount of time at the activity. As you can see determining your caloric needs by this method can become rather tedious. Appendix "A" has a brief list of the amount of calories used for some activities.

An easier approach which is quite accurate is to decide whether you live a "sedentary," "moderately active," or "very active" life-style. People who live "sedentary" lives include students, teachers, clerks, and others who are active, but not athletically so. Individuals who are "moderately active" are people who participate in short periods of physical activity. Examples include athletes who are not training for marathons. "Very active" individuals include laborers, construction workers, and others who are very active throughout most of the day.

In order to determine how many calories you need throughout the day based upon your activity level, you first need to determine your BMR from your weight as we did above. Depending upon how active you are, you will add a certain percentage of your BMR as shown in table one below. Generally speaking, you need to determine your BMR and then add the amount of calories appropriate for your level of activity. If you are "sedentary," you require 30% of your overall BMR for your activity level alone, which you then need to add to your BMR to determine how many calories you will need. "Moderately" and "very active" are shown below.

Table One Your overall caloric needs determined by your weight and activity level.

Lifestyle (overall activity level)	Calories based upon level of activity	Total daily caloric needs
Sedentary	30% of BMR	BMR+30 % of BMR
Moderately Active	40% of BMR	BMR+40 % of BMR
Very Active	50% of BMR	BMR+50 % of BMR

Let's work through some examples of how this works using the information from table one.

Example #1

A 32 year old woman who is a homemaker and weighs 145

pounds is trying to decide how many calories she can eat in a day without gaining weight. Depending upon the number of children she has, how old they are, and how helpful her husband is, she is probably "moderately active."

BMR = (145 pounds) (10 calories/pound) = 1,450 calories

Her caloric **activity needs** are 40% of her BMR because she is "moderately active." Because of this she requires an additional 580 calories above and beyond her BMR.

580 calories = (0.40) (1,450 calories)

Therefore, she needs 2,030 calories each day.

BMR	1,450 calories
+ Activity level	580 calories
Total daily calories:	2,030 calories

Notice that neither age nor gender were necessary to determine how many calories she would need daily, only her weight and activity level.

Example #2

In the second example, a 50 year old man who weighs 180 pounds works on a construction crew. His job demands a lot of physical labor and he is described as "very active." Because of his current weight, he will require 1,800 calories for his BMR on a daily basis.

BMR = (180 pounds) (10 calories/pound) = 1,800 calories

To determine his calorie needs based upon his activity alone, he will need to multiply his BMR by 50% (0.50) to discover that

15

he needs 900 calories in addition to his BMR needs.

$$900 \text{ calories} = (0.50) (1{,}800 \text{ calories})$$

Therefore, once we add his BMR needs and his activity level needs, we have determined that he needs 2,700 calories each day to maintain his current weight based upon his activity level.

BMR	1,800 calories
+ Activity level	900 calories
Total daily calories:	2,700 calories

Let's try one more example to illustrate several important points.

Example #3

The third person is also a 50 year old construction worker, but like the homemaker, he weighs 145 pounds. We know from the first case, that a person who weighs 145 pounds will need 1,450 calories a day as a result of his BMR.

$$BMR = (145 \text{ pounds}) (10 \text{ calories/pound}) = 1{,}450 \text{ calories}$$

The gentleman, like his colleague in the second example, is also a construction worker with a "very active" lifestyle based upon his job. However, because he weighs less than the 180 pound man, he only needs 725 calories for his level of activity.

$$725 \text{ calories} = (0.50) (1{,}450 \text{ calories})$$

Like the previous two examples, the total daily calorie requirement is the sum of BMR needs plus the calories needed for the level of activity. In this case, the 145 pound construction worker will need 2,175 calories each day to maintain his body weight.

16

BMR	1,450 calories
+ Activity level	725 calories
Total daily calories:	2,175 calories

By using the three examples above, several important points can be made. First, while the homemaker (example 1) and the construction worker (example 3) had different jobs, their BMR were the same because they both weighed 145 pounds. Based upon the difference in activity level, the construction worker needs about 145 more calories a day. This is roughly equivalent to one potato. Secondly, even though the two construction workers (examples 2 and 3) may have had identical jobs, the 180 pound man required 525 more calories than the 145 pound man, because of their weight difference.

YOUR CURRENT WEIGHT IS A MAJOR DETERMINANT OF HOW MANY CALORIES YOU NEED EACH DAY

These three examples show how the overall calories required by each person is more a function of the current weight than the activity level. This is an important concept when trying to determine how to lose weight. We shall soon see that the major benefit of exercise/work level is probably more related to toning the body and making it stronger, than to the actual consumption of calories.

Losing Weight

Numerous studies and many people have demonstrated that "crash" diets simply don't work. These types of diets are difficult for people to stay on for long periods of time and can be associated with severe metabolic problems. It has also been shown that people who "severely" restrict their daily calorie intake will potentially reduce their BMR making further weight reduction difficult. Much of the initial weight loss is probably more a result of water loss than fat. This, as too many people already know, can be extremely frustrating.

CRASH DIETS FREQUENTLY DON'T WORK AND CAN BE HARMFUL

It is important to remember that dietary changes need to be lifetime commitments and not "fad" diets with short-term goals. Quick fixes simply do not work. The best approach appears to be more of a long-term gradual weight reduction program designed to reduce your weight by approximately one pound a week. While initially the weight loss is not as impressive as quick weight loss programs, over the course of a year 52 pounds could be lost, hopefully never to be found again as long as dietary habits are maintained and you don't return to your old eating patterns. Once your desired weight (appendix B) has been reached, the goal then becomes one of maintaining weight without falling back into the old habits which resulted in the initial weight and lipid problems which can place people at an increased risk for heart disease and a heart attack.

How many calories can you eat and still lose weight?

If you are going to lose one pound of fat (adipose tissue) a week, you will have to either use an additional 3,477 calories a week (see how long and far you would have to run to reach this goal), or eat 3,477 fewer calories per week. Obviously, a combination of the two is possible, although the major contribution will undoubtedly come from eating fewer calories. In other words, you are what you eat. If you eat more than you need, you will gain weight. If you eat less than you need, you can lose weight as long as you don't change your BMR by major changes in your calorie intake, effecting the metabolism of your body and possibly doing more harm than good.

Let's look at how many calories each of the three people in the examples above needed to maintain their current body weight.

Table Two Daily caloric needs for three different people based upon their weight and activity level.

Example	Daily Caloric Needs
32 yr homemaker (145 pounds)	2,030
50 yr laborer (180 pounds)	2,700
50 yr laborer (145 pounds)	2,175

Adipose (fat) tissue is made up of 85% fat and 15% water. There are approximately 3,477 calories for each pound of fat on our body. This means that if you want to lose one pound of fat you either need to use up 3,477 more calories than you eat, eat 3,477 fewer calories than you need, or a combination of the two. Since we are looking at loosing one pound a week, then we need to eat approximately **500 fewer calories** than we need, **each day** of the week to lose one pound during that week.

$$496.7 \text{ calories/day} = \frac{3,477 \text{ calories/week}}{7 \text{ days/week}}$$

Eating 500 fewer calories a day would be equal to 1-2/3 rd beef or pork tacos with 2 ounces (oz) of beef or pork, two cups of beef stew, 4 oz of barbecued chicken, 5 oz of American processed cheese or swiss cheese, or 13-1/2 peaches. Clearly the peaches are better for you.

Alternatively, if you weigh 150 (appendix A) pounds, you could use an additional 3,477 calories a week by *sawing* wood for 7-1/2 hours or running at a speed of 5.3 miles an hour for one hour, six times a week. There aren't many people I know who could lose weight by doing this. It takes a lot more work to burn up calories than it does to push yourself away from the table and eat fewer calories.

> **A GOOD EXERCISE TO USE TO LOSE WEIGHT IS TO PUSH YOURSELF AWAY FROM THE TABLE**

For the three people we have been looking at during this chapter, each one could reduce their weight by an average of one pound a week if they continue their current activity levels and restrict the daily calorie intake as shown in table three below.

Table Three Changes in calorie intake necessary to reduce weight by an average of one pound in seven days.

Example	Daily Caloric Needs	Daily Caloric Needs to Lose one pound per week
32 yr homemaker (145 pounds)	2,030	1,530
50 yr laborer (180 pounds)	2,700	2,200
50 yr laborer (145 pounds)	2,175	1,675

Finally, it is important to remember that while you are losing weight, your BMR and activity level needs will also be decreasing. Fortunately, this weight loss will occur gradually allowing you time to gradually reduce the number of calories you are eating, without making major changes once you have begun a weight loss program. While some readers might enjoy the challenge of calculating their calorie needs from week to week, I have included a table (appendix C) for those people who would like to concentrate on losing the weight, rather than losing their minds doing the calculations.

There are a number of reasons why people do not tend to lose weight as rapidly as others. Some of these problems include, but are not limited to, variations in basal metabolic rates, incorrect estimate of activity level, hidden calories in the diet not frequently counted or remembered, and eating later in the day when calories cannot be used before being stored as fat for a "rainy day." It is also important to remember that weight loss does not always appear to occur evenly over time. The concept of "plateaus" has been used to describe a phenomena which is a problem for many people, but is not yet well understood. Plateaus represent a failure to lose weight (no change, hence the term plateau) despite your eating fewer calories than you theoretically need. Several theories exist about why this happens, including possible metabolic changes which might occur. While not fully understood, these plateaus can be rather frustrating and frequently result in people giving up and returning to their old dietary habits. One word of encouragement—persistence tends to pay off.

**LOSING WEIGHT MAY LOWER YOUR BMR FROM
10 TO 7 CALORIES PER POUND**

Even while this book is being written, new information is being published which demonstrated that weight loss of 10% or more can in some people reduce their BMR resulting in their needing only 7 to 8 calories for every pound of body weight instead of 10 calories. If this is true and you are one of these individuals, you may need to make further reductions in the number of calories you eat each day to reach your desired weight.

The Nutritional Content of Proteins, Carbohydrates, and Fats

In the first chapter of this book we looked at how cholesterol and fats are made and handled by our bodies. In the second chapter we looked at how we can determine how many calories we need each day to either maintain or lose weight. We will now turn our attention to the sources of these calories, proteins, carbohydrates, fat, and cholesterol.

Proteins

Although many people don't think about it there are several sources of proteins in our diet besides meat or meat products. For the purpose of this book we will define meat as:

> ANYTHING THAT MOVED UNDER ITS
> OWN POWER WHEN IT WAS ALIVE

This includes, but is not limited to, beef, chicken, turkey, fish, snails (escargot), squid (calamari), buffalo, polar bear, antelope, frogs (frog legs), beetles, deer, whale, shark, etc. You get the point, meat is not limited to hamburger and steaks. Interestingly enough, one of the frequent questions I get asked in my practice is, "If I can only have meat 2 or 3 times a week, how often can I have fish and chicken?"

> ## MEAT IS ANYTHING THAT MOVED UNDER ITS OWN POWER WHEN IT WAS ALIVE

Protein is an essential part of our diets. It is necessary to allow us to respond to stress, heal wounds, respond to infections, and many other functions. Adults need approximately 0.9 grams of protein for every kilogram of ideal body weight. Since there are 2.2 pounds for every kilogram (kg), we need 0.4 grams (gm) of protein for every pound (lb) we weigh.

$$0.4 \text{ gm protein/lb} = (0.9 \text{ gm protein/kg})(1 \text{ kg/2.2 lb})$$

This represents 15 percent of your total calories each day. For example, if you weigh 145 pounds and are "moderately active" (see Chapter 2, example #1), you need 2,030 calories per day. If 15% of your calories come from protein sources, then 304 calories each day should come from protein.

$$304 \text{ protein calories/day} =$$

$$(2,030 \text{ calories/day})(0.15 \text{ protein calories/calories})$$

For protein, there are approximately 4 calories for every gram. Since there are 304 protein calories in the above example, then this person needs 76 grams of protein a day. Most people would consider this more than adequate.

$$76 \text{ gms protein/day} = (304 \text{ calories/day})(1 \text{ gm of protein/4 calories})$$

> ## YOU NEED 0.4 GRAM OF PROTEIN EACH DAY FOR EVERY POUND YOU WEIGH

How to Bypass Your Bypass

For the die-hard meat eaters reading this book I can almost hear you saying, "You see, you do need meat." Well not quite, what we need is "protein" and it doesn't mater where it comes from as long as it is protein. While everyone knows that meat and meat products, including but not limited to dairy products, are high in protein, they can also be high in saturated fat. Saturated fat isn't necessarily good for you, particularly if you already have high cholesterol and triglyceride levels. There are a number of foods which are both high in protein, but have little or no saturated fat. Below I have listed just a few.

lentils, dried beans, peas,
rice, oats, barley, millet,
skim milk, egg whites,
yogurt (skim milk), tofu, soybeans,
seeds (sesame, pumpkin, sunflower, etc.), and nuts

> APPROXIMATELY 15 PERCENT OF YOUR
> CALORIES SHOULD BE FROM PROTEIN

There is antidotal evidence that diets too low in protein may result in overeating in an attempt to fulfill the protein needs of the body. There is also some evidence to suggest that soy protein may lessen menopausal symptoms, and reduce the incidence of Alzheimer's disease—although these reports are yet to be supported. Later in this book, we will look at specific foods and compare their protein, carbohydrate, fat, and calorie contents.

Carbohydrates

Carbohydrates consist of those foods which are primarily composed of sugar, starch, and fiber. Carbohydrates have fewer calories than proteins or fats (table 1) and are not (for most people) absolutely necessary for life because they can be made by the liver from proteins. Most diets designed to reduce cholesterol and fat intake recommend that 60-70% of your calories consist of carbohydrates. Like most things, too much isn't good either. If consumed in too great a quantity, these calories add up and weight gain occurs with associated increases in fats and eventually cholesterol. Carbohydrates have approximately 4 calories for every gram eaten. If we continue to look at the needs of a 145 pound "moderately active" person and ask how many calories will be needed each day, we discover that 1,421 calories are needed daily in the form of carbohydrates.

1,421 carbohydrate calories/day =

(2,030 calories/day) (0.70 carbohydrate calories/calories)

Since there are 4 calories for every gram (gm) of carbohydrate present in our diet, this person will need to eat approximately 355 grams of carbohydrate foods each day.

355 grams of carbohydrates/day =

(1,421 carbohydrate calories/day)(1 gram/4 calories)

Many of the foods which are high in carbohydrates also tend to be low in protein and fat. These foods are typically referred to as "heart healthy" and primarily include fruits, vegetables, and grains. Exceptions to this would be olives and avocados which are high in fat.

APPROXIMATELY 70 PERCENT OF YOUR CALORIES SHOULD BE FROM CARBOHYDRATES

Fats

Triglycerides are primarily made up of fats. As we discovered in chapter one, fats/triglycerides are an important part of the process of making cholesterol, whether they are consumed in the diet or made by your liver. Table one from chapter one showed that approximately 45% of all people with elevated lipid levels have a Type IV hyperlipidemia, which means that they have high triglycerides (fats) levels in their blood.

When compared to proteins and carbohydrates, fats have more than twice as many calories. Each gram of fat contributes approximately 9 calories to your daily intake. As we will see later in the book, there are three types of fats; 1) saturated fat, 2) monounsaturated fat, and 3) polyunsaturated fat. However, each type has the same number of calories.

WE NEED 7.5 GRAMS OF LINOLEIC ACID EACH DAY IN OUR DIET

We need 7.5 grams of linoleic acid in our daily diet to respond to infections and make the membranes for the cells of our body. This "essential fatty acid" is **the only "fat" we need** and is typically obtained with a diet that has a 10-15% fat content. Using the same example we have been using for proteins and carbohydrates, this person will need 304 calories from fat each day.

304 fat calories/day =

(2,030 calories/day) (0.15 fat calories/calories)

However, since there are more than twice as many calories in a gram of fat as a gram of protein, only 38 grams of fat will be needed compared with the 76 grams of protein necessary to provide the same number of calories.

37.7 grams of fat/day =

(304 fat calories/day) (1 gram fat/9 fat calories)

To further illustrate this point, if this person actually ate the same amount of fat as protein, they would eat an additional 38.3 grams of fat, which would increase the calorie intake by approximately 345 calories a day.

$$345 \text{ calories/day} = (38.3 \text{ grams/fat}) (9 \text{ calories/gram})$$

Over the course of ten days this person would have gained approximately one pound (3,477 calories) and over the course of a year would weigh about 36 pounds more than at the beginning of the year.

THERE ARE MORE CALORIES IN FAT THAN PROTEIN OR CARBOHYDRATES

Table one shows the number of calories present in each gram of protein, carbohydrate, fat, and alcohol, as well as the percentage of each type needed daily.

Table One Dietary calories in different types of foods.

Nutrient	Calories per gram	Percent Needed Daily
alcohol	7.0	0
carbohydrates	4.1	70
protein	5.65	15
fat (for linoleic acid)	9.35	15

Many people forget, or chose not to remember, the number of calories they consume in alcoholic beverages. Given the number of calories in alcohol, it is much more like a fat than anything else. Lite beer is beer that has had some of the carbohydrates and alcohol removed to reduce the number of calories present. For example, "regular" beer has an average of 146 calories in 12 ounces.

How to Bypass Your Bypass

The same amount of light beer has about 100 calories. To accomplish this reduction in calories all of the carbohydrates and protein have to be removed and some of the alcohol. If the carbohydrates and proteins were left in then 6.6 grams of alcohol would have been removed to reduce the calories to 100 in 12 ounces.

6.6 grams of alcohol =

(1 gram alcohol/7 calories) (46 calories)

The only way to reduce calories in a food or beverage is to remove them, like the example shown above for alcohol. Many foods prepared today have had their fat removed or reduced to significantly decrease the number of calories and the amount of fat present. Foods which are high in protein and fats also tend to be high in cholesterol. When people increase: 1) the amount of fat in their diet, particularly their saturated fats, 2) their cholesterol intake and/or 3) their overall number of calories (regardless of the source), the total cholesterol and LDL cholesterol will increase. We will learn more about the different types of fats in the next chapter.

In this chapter we have learned about protein, carbohydrates, and fats. We looked at some of the reasons why we might need them in our diet as well as how they contribute to our overall dietary intake of calories. In order to determine how many calories you need from each of the three categories, you need only to use the following steps. First, determine how many calories you need based upon your current weight and activity level as we discussed in the last chapter and as summarized in appendix C at the end of this book. Then you need to determine how many calories (15%) in fat, carbohydrates (70%) and proteins (15%) you need using table one above. This can be overwhelming at times (particularly as you start) but not impossible if you follow the step by step instructions and the examples in this chapter.

Learning More about Fats

F at, or adipose tissue as it is called in medicine, is one of the primary methods for storing energy in the body for future needs. It also serves to insulate our bodies from changes in temperature, cushion many areas of our bodies, effect hormone levels, and many other purposes. An average person might easily have 18% body fat. For a 145 pound person, this would equal 26.1 pounds. Since each pound represents approximately 3,477 calories (chapter 2), this represents more than 90,000 stored calories.

90,750 calories =

(3,477 calories/pound of fat) (26.1 pounds of fat)

This is more than enough calories to see you through a "rainy day." In fact, for this 145 pound person, it would see them through 45 "rainy days."

> ALMOST 1/2 OF AMERICANS 30 YEARS OR
> OLDER ARE OVERWEIGHT

However, too much fat can pose a substantial health risk by elevating your cholesterol and triglyceride levels, increasing the daily wear and tear of your joints, increasing the work on your heart, and decreasing the length of your life. In the United States it has been estimated that as much as 45% of the population over age 30 is obese, and as we discovered in chapter one, more than 90% of the people over age 30 have disease in the arteries of their heart. After reading chapters two and three you probably already recognize the major problem as one of overeating, and to an extent, under exercising. In this chapter we are going to look at the different types of fat present in our diets, some of the foods they are found in, and how different types of fat have different potential health risks.

THERE ARE THREE TYPES OF FATS: SATURATED, MONOUNSATURATED, AND POLYUNSATURATED

Examples of Foods High in
Saturated Fatty Acids and Cholesterol

bacon fat	beef fat	butter	chicken fat
cocoa butter	cream	ice cream	coconut
clotted cream	eggs	egg yolk	ham fat
whole-milk	lamb fat	solids	coconut oil
palm kernel oil	pork fat	lard	vegetable oil
vegetable	hydrogenated	turkey fat	
shortening	vegetable oil	whole-milk	
		solids	

Both monounsaturated and polyunsaturated fatty acids are frequently listed together because foods which have one, typically have the other. The polyunsaturated fatty acids which we need are called "essential fatty acids" because they are essential in making the cells of our bodies and controlling infections. Specifically, it is the linoleic acid found in polyunsaturated sources that we require. As mentioned in chapter three we need approximately 7.5 grams of linoleic acid daily.

THE ONLY FAT WE NEED IN OUR DIET IS LINOLEIC ACID, WHICH CAN BE FOUND IN VEGETABLE OILS

The substitution of polyunsaturated fatty acids for saturated fatty acids in the diet has been shown to be beneficial in the overall reduction of cholesterol. This is particularly true when the polyunsaturated to saturated ratio increases from 0.3 to 1.0, meaning that there has been an increase in the polyunsaturated fat eaten and a decrease in the saturated fat eaten, without increasing the total amount of fat eaten. Each of these fatty acids are oils and not solid at room temperature. Some examples are listed below.

Examples of Monounsaturated Oils/Fats
(oleic acid)

canola oil (rapeseed oil)
peanut oil
olive oil
sunflower oil
safflower oil

Examples of Polyunsaturated Oils/Fats
(linoleic acids/omega-6)

safflower oil
sunflower oil
corn oil
soybean oil

Examples of omega-3 oils
catfish, flounder, haddock, herring, mackerel,
orange roughy, perch, pike, salmon,
snapper, sturgeon, trout, shellfish

SATURATED FATS ARE SOLID AT ROOM TEMPERATURE

All naturally occurring polyunsaturated and monounsaturated fatty acids are "cis-fatty acids." These are kinked which reduce their tendency to pack tightly, increase their tendency to be liquids at room temperature, and are less associated with elevations in cholesterol. "Trans-fatty acids" are made when polyunsaturated oils are "hydrogenated" as part of the processing of foods, they are **never** naturally occurring. These are straighter and tend to become solid at room temperature. As a result they behave more like "saturated" fats and can also be bad for you.

In the past several years considerable controversy has centered around a debate as to whether margarine (partially hydrogenated) is better for you than butter. Initially it was thought that butter was much worse because of its cholesterol and saturated fatty acids which we know increases cholesterol levels. However, margarine can also be a problem because it may have up to 47% of its polyunsaturated bonds in a "trans" configuration. The higher the percent of "trans" bonds, the easier it is to store at room temperature, but the more it behaves like a saturated fat. Clearly the use of butter or hydrogenated vegetable products can both be bad for you, leading to increases in your cholesterol level. Table one shows some examples of hydrogenation ("trans-fatty acids") which occur during food processing and preparation.

Table One Hydrogenation ("trans-fatty acids") of food increases the shelf life, but may decrease ours.

Food	Maxium % "Trans" Configuration (Hydrogenation)	Effect of Hydrogenation on the Food
Processed Oils	17	prevent yellowing
Margarine	47	hardens at room temperature
Vegetable shortening	58	usable as a paste

The impact on our diet of hydrogenated foods can be clearly seen from table two which compares dietary fat changes over a sixty year period. Not only has the amount of fat changed in the American diet, but the processed fats have increased.

> **AMERICANS ARE EATING MORE SATURATED FATS THAN EVER BEFORE**

Table Two A comparison of American diets between 1910 and 1972.

Year	Fat grams/ day	Grams "trans" fatty acids/day	% "trans-fatty acids" of total fat intake
1910	125	4.4	3.5%
1972	155	12.1	7.8%

In the course of 60 years there has been a 20% increase in the amount of fat present in the American diet and a 175% increase in processed fat which can behave like saturated fats. While we need a certain amount of linoleic acid in our diet, the majority of changes in the American diet since the beginning of this century have been an increase in the number of calories we eat, an increase in the amount of fat we eat, an increase in the amount of processed fat we eat, a decrease in the physical labor we do, an increase in the number of obese people, an increase in cholesterol and triglyceride (fat) levels, and an increase in the number of deaths due to coronary artery disease. In the next two chapters we will look at how to read food labels to determine how much fat and cholesterol we are getting in our diet.

Learning to Read Food Labels

Because the number of calories per gram of protein, carbo-hydrates, and fats are different, the percentage of fat in food and the percentage of calories from fat in any food are two different things.

% OF FAT DOES NOT EQUAL % OF CALORIES FROM FAT

It is also important to realize that the fat and cholesterol content are two different things. As a result of consumer concerns, many food labels now show both the percentage of fat and the total fat calories present in a serving, as well as the cholesterol content. For example, peanut butter usually has no cholesterol but can be extremely high in fat. Let's look at an example of a peanut butter food label to illustrate this point.

Example # 1

The following label was found on a popular brand of peanut butter with a serving size of two tablespoons. This means that the number of calories and amount of fat, carbohydrates, and protein listed is the amount found in just two tablespoons of peanut butter.

Serving size: 2 tablespoons (36 grams)
Calories per serving: 190, Fat calories 100

Total Fat: 12 gram,   19 %
  Saturated Fat: 2.5 grams,   12 %
Cholesterol: 0 milligrams
Sodium: 200 milligrams
Total carbohydrates: 13 grams
  Fiber: 1 grams
  Sugars: 3 grams
Protein: 9 grams

The label shows that for a diet consisting of 2,000 calories, this two tablespoon serving gives you 19% of your recommended daily fat intake. This is the % of **Fat**, not the % of **Calories from Fat**. This is not what I consider an extremely healthy recommendation because if 12 grams represents 19 percent of your recommended intake of fat for every 2,000 calories, then you are being advised to eat 63.15 grams of fat for each 2,000 calories.

$$63.15 \text{ grams of fat} = (12 \text{ grams}/0.19)$$

Since there are approximately 9 calories for every gram of fat, you will be eating 568.35 fat calories for each 2,000 calories you consume.

$$568.35 \text{ fat calories} =$$

$$(9 \text{ calories}/\text{gram of fat}) (63.15 \text{ grams of fat})$$

This is a diet with 30% fat. Although this is better than the typical American diet it is still far from ideal.

30% fat calories = (568.35 calories/2000 calories)

Please notice however, that this represents the % of fat calories and as I mentioned at the beginning of the chapter:

% OF FAT DOES NOT EQUAL % OF CALORIES FROM FAT

Please look at the second line on the label which states: "Calories per serving: 190, Fat calories 100." This means that of the 190 calories present in the two tablespoon serving of peanut butter, 100 of these are fat calories. This means that 52.6% of the calories in the two tablespoons of peanut butter are fat. The 19% total fat (12 grams) quoted on the label is the percentage of your recommended fat intake for the day based upon a diet which has 2,000 calories. It is not the percent of **Calories** from **Fat** that you get in those two tablespoons, and that is why the fat calories and total calories are both important to look at when reading the label.

$$52.6 \text{ \% of all calories are fat calories } = \frac{100 \text{ fat calories}}{190 \text{ total calories}}$$

In other words, more than half of the calories are fat calories and it's no wonder the average American diet is 42% fat. The label also tells us that there is absolutely no cholesterol in the peanut butter. Have you ever wondered that if something has no cholesterol then how it can be bad for you? The answer is simple, **fat and cholesterol are two different things**.

FAT AND CHOLESTEROL ARE TWO DIFFERENT THINGS

The connection between fat and cholesterol is that the liver makes the two as described in chapter one. The label also showed that there are 2.5 grams of saturated fat in each serving and a lot (200 mg sodium) of salt. Finally, here's the bad news, this brand of peanut butter was "reduced fat"—the regular version has 63.5

percent fat calories.

$$63.5 \% = \frac{153 \text{ fat calories}}{241 \text{ total calories}}$$

This first example showed why it is important to look at the entire food label and how to determine the percentage of calories (52.6%) from fat, as well as what percent (19%) of necessary fat calories for the day come from one serving of the peanut butter. It also showed us that there can be absolutely no cholesterol in a food which is loaded with fat—in this case saturated fat. Now let's look at a food that is relatively healthy for us.

DON'T BE FOOLED BY THE FOOD LABEL

Example # 2

This second example was found on a can of vegetable soup with beef "stock." It is important to point out that the number of calories, percentages and absolute quantities of food listed on the label are for each serving size. Most containers of food have more than one serving in them so that if you eat more than one serving (1/2 cup in this example) you will be eating more calories and fat. It is helpful to use scales and measuring cups to help you determine the actual serving size. Too many people have uncounted calories because they have larger servings than the ones listed on the package and then wonder why they can't lose weight or reduce their cholesterol.

When reading a food label, like anything else in life, its good to have a basic plan of action. You may want to start by asking four primary questions:

1) How big is the serving size and how many calories are present in one serving?

2) How many of the calories are in the form of fat and how many grams of fat are present for each serving? Including what type (saturated, polyunsaturated, and monounsaturated) of fat is present.

3) How much cholesterol is present in each serving?

4) How much sodium (salt) is present?

Vegetable soup with beef broth
Serving size: 1/2 cup condensed soup
Calories per serving: 90,   Fat calories 10

Total Fat: 1 gram,   2 %
  Saturated Fat: 0 grams,   0 %
Cholesterol: 5 milligrams
Sodium: 750 milligrams
Total carbohydrates: 17 grams
  Fiber: 2 grams
  Sugars: 8 grams
Protein: 3 grams

THERE ARE FOUR BASIC QUESTIONS TO ASK WHEN READING A FOOD LABEL

The first question is almost always straight forward. In this case a serving is one-half cup and there are 90 calories in that 1/2 cup of soup. The second question is also easily answered if you don't get confused by the different numbers thrown at you by the label. Remember just because something is printed on the label doesn't always mean it's helpful. In this case the percentages across from the "total fat" on the label is not needed to answer the question. One-half cup of soup has 1 gram of total fat and 0 grams of saturated fat. The percent of calories from fat in one serving is 11 percent.

$$11.1 \% = \frac{10 \text{ fat calories}}{90 \text{ total calories}}$$

The third and fourth questions are also easily answered from the food labels, there are 5 milligrams of cholesterol and 750 milligrams of sodium for every 1/2 cup serving. An important point to remember about many canned foods is that they typically have a significant amount of sodium (salt) present to preserve the food.

As you can see, this can of soup is relatively good for you with only 90 calories, of which 11% are fat (no saturated fat) and only 5 milligrams of cholesterol. The only significant drawback is the amount of salt.

Example # 3

Many different types of crackers are available today as compared with 40 or 50 years ago. We're going to look at two different types of crackers in the next two examples. The first type

Serving size: 5 crackers (15 grams)
Calories per serving: 70,   Fat calories 20

Total Fat: 2.5 gram, 4%
  Saturated Fat: 0.5 grams,   2%
Cholesterol: 0 milligrams
Sodium: 135 milligrams
Total carbohydrates: 11 grams
  Fiber: 0 grams
  Sugars: 1 grams
Protein: 1 grams

(example 3) is a "reduced fat" variety, while example 4 is not. We will first answer the basic four questions for each type of cracker and then do a comparison.

The "reduced fat" cracker has a serving size of five crackers which have 70 calories—this means that there are 14 calories for every cracker you eat. These five crackers have almost as many calories as in the 1/2 cup of soup, although there is considerably more fat in the crackers with 20 of the 70 calories being fat calories. This means that almost 29 % of the calories are from fat.

$$28.6\ \% \ = \ \frac{20 \text{ fat calories}}{70 \text{ total calories}}$$

Remember that this is for only five crackers. If you eat 10 or 15 crackers (not hard to do), you will get two or three times as many calories and fat. Unlike the soup, the fat present in the crackers is 20 percent "saturated" fat:

$$20\% \text{ saturated fat} = \frac{0.5 \text{ mg saturated fat}}{2.5 \text{ mg total fat}}$$

Like the peanut butter example there is no cholesterol, so they could be marketed as zero cholesterol crackers. While this makes many people believe they are eating "heart healthy," not many calories, no cholesterol, etc., they are actually eating a substantial amount of fat and calories for only five crackers. Finally, there are 135 milligrams of salt "per five cracker serving." Let's contrast this to a cracker which is not labeled "reduced fat".

Example # 4

Like the "reduced fat" cracker, there are only 70 calories per serving. However, now the serving size is only four crackers versus the five crackers for the "reduced fat" variety. An obvious difference between the two types of crackers can be seen in the percent of calories from fat. For these four crackers almost 36% of the calories come from fat.

$$35.7 \% = \frac{25 \text{ fat calories}}{70 \text{ total calories}}$$

One-third is saturated fat.

$$33.3\% \text{ saturated fat} = \frac{1 \text{ mg saturated fat}}{3 \text{ mg total fat}}$$

Serving size: 4 crackers (14 grams)
Calories per serving: 70,   Fat calories 25

Total Fat: 3 gram,   5 %
 Saturated Fat: 1 grams, 5 %
Cholesterol: 0 milligrams
Sodium: 160 milligrams
Total carbohydrates: 9 grams
 Fiber: <1 grams
 Sugars: 1 grams
Protein: 1 grams

There is no cholesterol in these crackers, just a lot of fat. There is also more salt in one serving (160 milligrams) of these crackers than the "reduced fat" cracker.

The differences between the two types of crackers may not seem like much at first glance and neither cracker are what you would call nutritious, but let's do a comparison. Suppose you ate 20 crackers, what would be the difference between the amount of calories and fat you would be eating?

Table One A comparison between "reduced fat" and "regular" crackers.

Type of Craker	Number of Crackers	Total Calories	Total Fat Calories	Grams of Fat	Grams of Saturated Fat
Reduced Fat	20	280	80	10	2
Regular	20	350	125	15	5

For a 170 pound person with a "moderately active" lifestyle (appendix C) trying to lose one pound a week, you need to reduce your total number of calories to 1,883 calories a day. If only 15% of these calories come from fat, this represents approximately 282 fat calories.

$$282 \text{ fat calories/day} = (0.15) \, (1{,}883 \text{ calories/day})$$

This means that eating 20 of these "reduced fat" crackers just provided you with 1/3 the fat calories you needed for the day, without giving you the type of fat (chapter three) you need. As long as you eat only one serving there doesn't appear to be much difference, but once you eat a few more the differences add up.

Example # 5

Let's conclude our reading of food labels by comparing 2% and skim milk. Whole milk is approximately 3.2% fat, so the reduction to 2% is a slight improvement. In an 8 oz glass of 2% milk there are 120 calories, of which 37.5% of the calories are coming from fat.

$$37.5 \% = \frac{45 \text{ fat calories}}{120 \text{ total calories}}$$

How to Bypass Your Bypass

Of this, 70% of the fat calories are saturated fat.

$$70\% \text{ saturated fat} = \frac{3.5 \text{ gm saturated fat}}{5 \text{ gm total fat}}$$

> Serving size: 8 oz of 2 % milk
> Calories per serving:120,   Fat calories 45
>
> Total Fat: 5 gram,   8 %
>   Saturated Fat: 3.5 grams,   18 %
> Cholesterol: 25 milligrams
> Sodium: 110 milligrams
> Total carbohydrates: 11 grams
>   Fiber: 0 grams
>   Sugars: 11 grams
>   Protein: 8 grams

Like all milk products, cholesterol is present. In this case there are 25 milligrams of cholesterol. There are also 110 milligrams of salt in an 8 oz glass of 2% milk. Surprised!! Cottage cheese and milk shakes are also loaded with salt.

> Serving size: 8 oz of skim milk
> Calories per serving:80,   Fat calories 0
>
> Total Fat: 0 gram,   0 %
>   Saturated Fat: 0 grams,   0 %
> Cholesterol: 5 milligrams
> Sodium: 110 milligrams
> Total carbohydrates: 11 grams
>   Fiber: 0 grams
>   Sugars: 11 grams
>   Protein: 8 grams

In the same amount of skim milk there are 80 calories and no fat. As we will see in chapter nine, skim milk is not totally fat free. There is one-fifth the amount of cholesterol in skim milk as there is in 2% milk and the same amount of sodium/salt.

$$20\% = \frac{5 \text{ mg cholesterol (skim)}}{25 \text{ mg cholesterol (2\%)}}$$

Sample Meals

Using the information from the example labels shown above we can determine how many calories, fat, and cholesterol we would eat if we had we had one of three different meals. The first meal includes an 8 oz glass of 2% milk, a cup of vegetable soup with beef broth, and 20 "regular" crackers with two tablespoons of "reduced fat" peanut butter. The second meal consists of 8 oz of skim milk, a cup of vegetable soup with beef broth, 20 "reduced fat" crackers, and two tablespoons of "reduced fat" peanut butter. The final meal has 8 oz of skim milk, a cup of the same vegetable soup, 5 "reduced fat" crackers (one serving), and no peanut butter.

Meal One

Food	Total Calories	Total Fat Calories	Grams of Fat	Grams of Saturated Fat	Total Cholesterol
2% milk	120	45	5	3.5	25
soup	180	20	2	0	5
crackers	350	125	15	5	0
peanut butter	190	100	12	2.5	0
Total	840	290	34	11	30

34.5 % of the total calories are fat calories

$$= \frac{290 \text{ fat calories}}{840 \text{ total calories}}$$

Meal Two

Food	Total Calories	Total Fat Calories	Grams of Fat	Grams of Saturated Fat	Total Cholesterol
skim milk	80	0	0	0	5
soup	180	20	2	0	5
crackers	280	80	10	2	0
peanut butter	190	100	12	2.5	0
Total	730	200	24	4.5	10

27.4% of the total calories are fat calories

$$= \frac{200 \text{ fat calories}}{730 \text{ total calories}}$$

Meal Three

Food	Total Calories	Total Fat Calories	Grams of Fat	Grams of Saturated Fat	Total Cholesterol
skim milk	80	0	0	0	5
soup	180	20	2	0	5
crackers	70	20	2.5	0.5	0
Total	330	40	4.5	0.5	10

12.1% of the total calories are fat calories

$$= \frac{40 \text{ fat calories}}{330 \text{ total calories}}$$

By reducing the number of crackers eaten, drinking skim milk, and eliminating the peanut butter, we not only reduced the number of calories in this meal from 840 to 330, but we decreased the fat eaten from 34.5% to 12.1% of the total calories.

When looking at food labels it is important to look carefully at the serving size and the percent of fat calories present in each serving. An example of how to read food labels is shown in appendix D along with step by step instructions. It must be emphasized that cholesterol and fat are not the same thing, although they are related as we saw in chapter one. In the next chapter we will look at cholesterol and some of the foods which are relatively high in cholesterol.

What is Cholesterol?

C holesterol is an animal steroid whose chemical structure is shown in figure one. While it is not the purpose of this book to turn the reader into a chemist, it is probably important to have some idea of what cholesterol and fatty acids look like chemically so you can see that there is an obvious difference between the two. You don't need to know what the symbols mean to see that they look totally different. Figure one also shows what a fatty acid looks like. If three fatty acids are linked together by glycerol, you get a "**tri-glyceride**" which help make up fat. The -OH sticking out of the cholesterol molecule means that cholesterol is not only a steroid, but it is also an alcohol.

Most of the cholesterol in our bodies make up membranes (outer walls) that hold the cells of our bodies together and help to control what goes in and out of our cells. Only about 7 % of the cholesterol present in our bodies is actually found in the blood. Our liver is capable of making all the cholesterol we need. Part of the cholesterol made by the liver (chapter one) becomes "bile salts" (bile) which is released from our gallbladder when we eat fat. This helps to digest and absorb the fat which then becomes

Figure one Molecular structure of cholesterol and fatty acid.

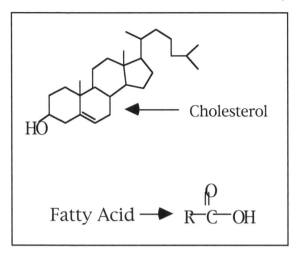

"chylomicrons" as we saw in chapter one.

OUR LIVER IS CAPABLE OF MAKING ALL
THE CHOLESTEROL WE NEED

Cholesterol is also important for making hormones in our body. This includes making sex (male and female) hormones, hormones (aldosterone) which regulate our salt level, adrenaline for responding to stress, and other chemicals. Because cholesterol cannot dissolve in water (blood) it must be attached to proteins to make *"lipo-proteins"* which are transported through the blood. They each have different names depending upon how much cholesterol, triglycerides, and protein they have. Depending upon the combination (chapter one, table two) of these ingredients they are given different names:

HDL cholesterol
LDL cholesterol
IDL cholesterol
VLDL cholesterol
Chylomicrons

These original names for the different types of cholesterol come from where they are found in a test tube of blood after it has been spun (centrifugation) for study in the laboratory. The heavier something is, the more toward the bottom of the test tube it is found. This is very similar to looking at a river and asking where you will find the sticks, leaves, mud, dirt, rocks, and fish. The heavier objects (rocks) will more likely be found at the bottom of the water, the lighter ones (leaves and branches) toward the surface, with everything else somewhere in between.

Likewise, after the blood has been spun, these different types of cholesterol are found in different layers of the blood as shown in figure two. The heaviest (HDL) will be found toward the bottom of the tube just like the rocks on the bottom of the river. The IDL cholesterol is less dense (heavy) and is found above the HDL layer. The very low density lipoprotein (VLDL) cholesterol is found near the top like the leaves and tree branches in a river, with the LDL layer in between the IDL and VLDL layers. The chylomicrons should be absent in the majority of people if they have been fasting. People with relatively large amounts of fats (VLDL and chylomicrons) can have blood which looks more like tomato soup than blood.

Figure two Location of different types of cholesterol in the test tube.

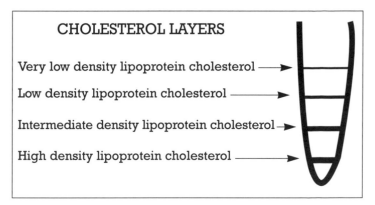

The recommendation from the American Heart Association is to reduce your cholesterol intake to less than 300 milligrams per day if you have elevated blood cholesterol because of its association with coronary artery disease. Currently, the average amount of cholesterol eaten by an American per day is 500 milligrams. People who eat eggs on a daily basis can easily eat more than 800 milligrams of cholesterol each day. Table one lists some of the common foods which have cholesterol and the approximate amount present.

Table one Amount of cholesterol in 100 grams of the following foods.

Food	Amount of Cholesterol (milligrams)
one egg	280*
butter	250
liver	300
meat (non-organ)	60-70
cheese	100

* this is the amount in an average egg yolk

When is my cholesterol level too high?

In the mid-1980s the physician cholesterol education faculty recommended that cholesterol levels greater than 200 milligrams per deciliter (mg/dl) were too high in individuals with more than one risk factor (appendix E) for coronary artery disease. The previous approach used the average cholesterol result as a guide to decide if a person's cholesterol level was high, low, or just right. However, the average cholesterol level of 248 mg/dl was also associated with 48% of the American population dying from heart disease. Clearly, the average result was not a good one. Table two shows that more than half of the US population has a total cholesterol greater than 220 mg/dl, with is associated with 85% of the excessive deaths from heart disease.

> IF YOU HAVE HEART DISEASE YOUR CHOLESTEROL
> IS TOO HIGH

Table Two Excess death from elevated cholesterol levels.

Total Cholesterol Level (mg/dl)	Percent of US Population	Percent of Excess Deaths from Heart Disease
< 220	45	15
220-310	50	75
> 310	5	10

Currently it is recommended that cholesterol levels be checked every five years if your cholesterol levels are "normal." The validity of testing your blood depends upon several factors. First you need to fast (not eat or drink anything except water) for at least 12 hours prior to having your blood drawn. Medications should probably be taken (with water only) and you should check with your doctor for his/her recommendations. Secondly, you should be sitting for several minutes before having the sample taken and the tourniquet should be on for as little time as possible to prevent incorrect results. It is important that you not be sick at the time of the test because this can result in incorrect results. For example, if you've had a myocardial infarction (heart attack) you may have artificially low levels of cholesterol for up to three months, which does not represent your true cholesterol levels. Similar problems can occur while you have an infection or if you are pregnant.

> 85% OF EXCESSIVE DEATHS FROM HEART
> DISEASE OCCUR IN PEOPLE WITH CHOLESTEROL
> LEVELS GREATER THAN 220 MG/DL

If your cholesterol levels are elevated, the current recommendations are focused on changing your diet and rechecking your cholesterol after six weeks, unless you are currently having heart problems. In work that I presented in the United States and in London (1995), as well as recent publications in medical journals (chapter eight), dietary changes are absolutely essential if a significant reduction in your cholesterol is to occur. Medications in the absence of dietary change did not significantly reduce people's cholesterol levels and just seeing your doctor won't magically improve things either.

DIETARY CHANGES ARE NECESSARY IF YOU EXPECT TO SEE MAJOR CHANGES IN YOUR CHOLESTEROL

Foods to definitely avoid if you're going to reduce your cholesterol

The foods listed near the top of table three are high in cholesterol and fat. Foods which are high in cholesterol and fat should be eliminated from your diet if you're trying to reduce your cholesterol levels. Also included in table three are other meats (fish, poultry, and shellfish) which have less cholesterol and fat. This assumes that these meats do not have additional fat or cholesterol added to them in the form of gravies, toppings, dressings, et cetera.

Table Three Cholesterol and fat content in 3 oz of various meats.

Meat	Milligrams of Cholesterol	Grams of Total Fat
Brains	1,746	10.7
Sweetbreads (pancreas)	400	2.8
Kidney	329	2.9

How to Bypass Your Bypass

Meat	Milligrams of Cholesterol	Grams of Total Fat
Liver	270	4.0
Shrimp	166	0.9
Heart	164	4.8
Veal	128	4.7
Oysters	93	4.2
Abalone	90	0.8
Blue Crab	85	1.5
Pork	79	11.1
Dark Chicken (no skin)	79	8.2
Lamb	78	8.8
Beef	77	8.7
Salmon	74	9.3
Dark Turkey (no skin)	72	6.1
White Chicken (no skin)	72	3.8
Lobster	61	0.5
White Turkey (no skin)	59	1.3
Clams	57	1.7
Light Tuna (no oil)	55	0.7
Alaskan king crab	45	1.3
Scallops	34	0.8

When dietary restrictions are followed closely, significant improvements in cholesterol levels can occur. Many investigators agree that by reducing your total cholesterol intake to less than

300 milligrams a day and by reducing your fat intake to less than 30% of your total calories, you can reduce your cholesterol by 30 to 40 mg/dl. Typically, this results in a 10 to 20% reduction in cholesterol which represents a 20 to 40% reduction in the risk of heart disease. Diets which focus on fruits and vegetables with vitamin supplementation have demonstrated reductions of 70 mg or more in some people.

SIGNIFICANT REDUCTIONS IN YOUR DIET CAN
RESULT IN MAJOR REDUCTIONS IN CHOLESTEROL

The addition of substitute egg products have allowed many individuals the luxury of having "egg" equivalents without the cholesterol. However, many diets fail because significant reductions in meat and egg intake does not occur or calorie intake increases (table four) by eating more breads, grains, cereals, and pasta to presumably make up for going without meat. The result of these excessive calories can be an increase in triglycerides which can lead to increased cholesterol levels. The end result is a diet which is not as effective as you need, resulting in further frustration.

Table Four The effect of cholesterol, fats, and excessive calories.

Food	Effect
Cholesterol	increases total and LDL cholesterol
Excessive Calories	increases total and LDL cholesterol, decreases HDL cholesterol
Saturated fats	increases total and LDL cholesterol

Understanding the Need for Minerals and Vitamins

Many people have compared the functioning of our bodies with that of a finely tuned automobile. One of the major differences between an auto mechanic and a physician is that physicians work on their patients while the motor is still running. Up to this point in our discussion on heart disease, diet, and cholesterol we have been looking at the major parts of the system and how they relate to each other. In this chapter we're going to look at what lubricates these different parts—what is necessary for them to work.

Our bodies are regulated by proteins called enzymes. Without them, many of the chemical reactions in our body either would not work or would be significantly slowed down. In fact, many of the medications used to help control cholesterol work by slowing down one of these enzymes, slowing but not stopping the production of cholesterol. In this chapter we will look at the vitamins and minerals necessary to run our bodies and help digest the proteins, carbohydrates, and fats we eat, turning them into the proteins, carbohydrates, and fats that we need to survive.

MEDICINES WORK BY INCREASING OR DECREASING OUR BODY'S NATURAL ABILITIES

Minerals and Vitamins

Several minerals have been identified which are essential for good health. The term essential is reserved for those nutrients which the body needs and cannot make. The eight essential amino acids (protein) and linoleic acid (only essential fat) can all be obtained from vegetables, vegetable oils, legumes, dairy products, fish, and meat. While many of the essential minerals can be found in meat, some cannot, and all of them can be found in foods other than meat. Table one lists many of these minerals and some of the foods where they can be found, along with some of the reasons we need them in our diet.

Table One Minerals essential in our diet.

Mineral	Source	Purpose
Calcium	dairy	bone, blood pressure
Copper	nuts, drinking water, legumes, shellfish, organ meats	nerves
Iodine	Iodized foods, fish, shellfish, dairy, some vegetables	thyroid hormone
Iron	meat, eggs, fish, green vegetables	hemoglobin for blood
Magnesium	vegetables, seafood, chocolate, nuts, grains, legumes	nerves and muscles

Mineral	Source	Purpose
Manganese	whole cereals, nuts, and fruits	control of fat and cholesterol
Phosphorus	most foods	nucleic acids, energy production, and cell membranes
Selenium	seafood, kidney, liver	heart and muscles
Zinc	oysters, herring, whole grains, nuts, liver	nucleic acids, wound healing, growth

Along with the dietary need for minerals, our bodies need a certain number of vitamins to work correctly. Failure to have sufficient vitamins in our diet can result in certain health problems. The vitamins consist of those which are fat-soluble and those which are water-soluble. In brief terms, the water soluble vitamins are easily removed from our body when we empty our bladder. However, the fat soluble vitamins, while necessary for optimal functioning of the body can be stored in the fat of the body when there is excess. Over time these excess stores may be harmful. Because of the differences in these two groups of vitamins, the water soluble vitamins are listed in table two and the fat soluble vitamins are shown in table three.

Table Two The essential water soluble vitamins.

Vitamin	Source	Purpose
Thiamine (B-1)	grains, pork, legumes, organ meat	helps remove carbon dioxide from body
Riboflavin (B-2)	many foods	energy production
Pyridoxine (B-6)	vegetables, whole grain cereals, meat	protein metabolism

Vitamin	Source	Purpose
Vitamin B-12	dairy, eggs, meat	nucleic acids
Ascorbic Acid (C)	citrus fruits, green peppers, tomato	bone and cartilage
Biotin	vegetables, legumes, meats	carbohydrate, protein, and fat metabolism
Choline	grains, legumes, liver, egg yolk	lipids and nerve function
Folacin	whole wheat, green, vegetables, legumes	nucleic acids and proteins
Niacin	grains, legumes, lean meats, and liver	oxidation-reduction reactions
Pantothenic acid	many foods	energy production

There are ten essential vitamins which are water soluble; of these only vitamin B-12 cannot be found in plants. For vegetarians who avoid meat, eggs, and dairy products, B-12 can be obtained either from cereal or vegetable protein fortified with B-12, or if necessary it can be obtained from vitamin supplements. Many of these vitamins are involved either in energy production and/or the breakdown of protein, carbohydrates, and fat in our diet. Several are involved in nucleic acids which make up our DNA (deoxyribonucleic acid) which makes up our genetic code.

> **STRICT VEGETARIANS SHOULD EITHER EAT CEREALS OR VEGETABLES FORTIFIED IN VITAMIN B-12 OR TAKE A VITAMIN SUPPLEMENT**

Severe health problems can occur if we do not get adequate supplies of these vitamins in our diet. These include scurvy, anemia, depression, pellagra, nausea, vomiting, diarrhea, fatigue, convulsions, muscle twitching, bleeding, and beriberi with associated nerve and heart problems. In addition to insufficient quantities of the water soluble vitamins, Vitamin B-6 has reportedly been shown to be toxic in doses exceeding 100 milligrams per day with the recommended daily intake of 2 milligrams per day.

Deficiencies in the fat soluble vitamins include night blindness which can progress to permanent blindness if too little vitamin A is present in the diet. Too much vitamin A can cause headaches, vomiting, anorexia, and swelling of arms and legs. Vitamin D is necessary for bone formation and if too little is in the diet of children rickets occur. In adults the bone becomes soft (osteomalacia) as calcium is lost from the bone. The importance of antioxidant vitamins like vitamin E has only recently been appreciated. It is possible to become anemic if too little is present in the body. Vitamin E is relatively non-toxic. If there is not enough vitamin K in the diet severe bleeding problems can occur. Toxicity is difficult but problems have been reported with man-made forms which have been known to cause jaundice.

Table Three The essential fat soluble vitamins.

Mineral	Source	Purpose
Vitamin A (retinol)	B-carotene in green vegetables, liver, carotenoids in yellow vegetables, milk, butter, cheese	vision, sugar production
Vitamin D	fortified milk, eggs, cod liver oil	growth and calcium absorption
Vitamin E	green leafy vegetables, seeds, margarines, wheat germ	antioxidant prevents cell damage

Mineral	Source	Purpose
Vitamin K	green leafy vegetables, peas, fruits, cereals, and meat	blood clotting

While the lists of essential vitamins and minerals include the major requirements for the body to perform optimally, there are undoubtedly other sources of these vitamins and minerals not listed here. Excesses and deficiencies can occur with almost anything and a good rule of thumb is moderation. If in doubt consult your doctor or pharmacist.

Antioxidant Vitamins

In recent years a considerable amount of information and misinformation has been published about three specific vitamins known as antioxidant vitamins. These are:

BETA-CAROTENE, VITAMIN C, & VITAMIN E

As shown in tables two and three, many foods contain these vitamins. These antioxidant vitamins neutralize the effects of "free radical" oxygen molecules which are produced by our bodies. The "free radicals" can damage genetic (DNA) material, cause skin and tissue damage, and cause problems with proteins, carbohydrates, and fats in our bodies. Some studies have linked "free radicals" with cancer, heart disease, arthritis, strokes, cataracts and Parkinson's disease. There is some evidence to suggest that nitroglycerin given to patients experiencing chest pain (angina) from the heart is having some of its effect by being a "free radical" oxygen scavenger.

Beta-carotene is also known as provitamin A. This is different from vitamin A as noted above in the fat soluble vitamins. Beta-carotene is not known to be toxic, while vitamin A can be.

Relatively high doses of beta-carotene have been thought to be helpful in protecting against heart disease, throat, and lung cancers and strokes.

Vitamin C has been reported to be good for decreasing symptoms from the common cold, and protective against cataracts and colon cancer. It has also been associated with minor increases the production of HDL cholesterol and decreasing blood pressure. Vitamin C also increases the absorption of iron in the diet.

The antioxidant effect of vitamin E has been touted as helping to reduce the oxidation of LDL cholesterol as mentioned in chapter one. It is also thought by some to improve the response to aging, and along with vitamin C, it is felt to improve wound healing.

ANTI-OXIDANT VITAMINS MAY BE HELPFUL IN HEART DISEASE, CANCER AND AGING

Some specific examples of foods which are good sources of antioxidant vitamins include, but are not limited to, the following foods. As you can see, many of the foods which provide approximately one-quarter of your daily needs for one of the vitamins may be a source of at least one other antioxidant vitamin.

Beta-carotene

Fruits (yellow to orange-yellow)
apricots, cantaloupe, carrots, mango, papaya, peaches

Vegetables (primarily green leafy)
beet greens, bok choy, broccoli, carrots, kale greens,
mustard greens, pumpkins, romaine lettuce,
spinach, sweet potato, sweet red pepper,

tomato, winter squash, yellow squash

Grains and Meats
fortified instant cereals, liver

Vitamin C

Fruits
cantaloupe, vitamin C enriched fruit juice (grapefruit,
orange, etc.), honeydew melon, kiwi, mango, oranges,
papaya, pineapple, raspberries, strawberries

Vegetables
asparagus, beet greens, bok choy, broccoli, cauliflower, brussels
sprouts, cabbage, cauliflower, green peppers, kale greens, mustard greens, potato (with skin), snow peas, spinach, sweet potato, sweet red pepper, tomato, tomato juice, turnip greens

Vitamin E

almonds, filberts, green leafy vegetables,
hazelnuts, peanut butter, shrimp, sunflower seeds,
vegetable oils, vitamin E fortified cereals

The essential vitamins and minerals needed by our bodies to optimally function are typically found in the variety of foods we eat. All but vitamin B-12 can be found in non-meat sources and the presence of B-12 fortified cereals and vegetable protein allow strict vegetarians an alternative to vitamin supplements. While diets with only meat might result in less than optimal intake of vitamin C, E, and folacin, fortunately most people do not eat just meat. As with any dietary change, the use of supplemental vitamins or mega-vitamins should be done with the approval of your physician.

How to Bypass Your Bypass

Along with our need for a certain number of calories derived from proteins, carbohydrates, and fat, we need certain vitamins and minerals if our body is to function optimally. Many changes in our diets can be accomplished without risking our health, due to excesses in most people's diets. It is also important that you drink a sufficient amount of water each day to meet your body's needs. For many people this means six to eight glasses of water each day. In the next chapter, we will see how recent studies have demonstrated the ability to reduce cholesterol and triglyceride levels without using medications.

How Changing Your Diet Can Change Your Cholesterol

The relationship between cholesterol and heart disease was considered early in the 20th century but was dismissed by many until the 1950-1960s. Studies looking at how cholesterol might be related to coronary artery disease began by looking at different types of monkeys. These animals were fed diets either high or low in cholesterol. When the arteries were looked at to see if cholesterol had built up after eating diets high in cholesterol, cholesterol deposits were seen. These arteries give the appearance of clogged pipes, except you can't use a plunger to unplug them. These deposits were less if the animals ate food low in cholesterol.

When we look at groups of people with little or no coronary artery disease we find that the cholesterol values can easily be below 150 milligrams/deciliter (mg/dl). As cholesterol levels increase the risk of heart disease increases dramatically, with a good rule of thumb being that for every 1% change in cholesterol there is a 2% change in the risk of heart disease. Since these initial animal studies, a large amount of attention has been focused on lowering cholesterol and triglycerides levels with medications.

How to Bypass Your Bypass

Some of the initial drugs have been removed from the market as more effective and less problematic medicines have been developed.

> **FOR EVERY 1% INCREASE IN CHOLESTEROL THERE IS A 2% INCREASED RISK OF HEART DISEASE**

Less attention has been focused on changing the dietary habits of people due to 1) difficulty getting people to change their eating habits despite significant life threatening health problems, 2) problems with inadequate numbers of physicians, dietitians, or nutritionists being training to accomplish the task, and 3) failure for insurers to pay for preventive treatment programs, as well as many additional reasons.

In fairness to the insurance industry, it is difficult to justify the cost of paying for health maintenance programs when a healthy individual can, after the benefit of dietary training with one company, leave the health plan for a second health insurance company. Clearly, the first company losses money while the patient reduces his/her health risk and the second insurer doesn't pay a dime. What we need is a setting where all health insurance companies cover preventive treatment of heart disease and other health problems.

In the 1980s attention started to focus on dietary changes, primarily in addition to drug treatment. The American Heart Association (AHA) made recommendations for dietary changes which reduced the consumption of fat and cholesterol in the diet. The two different diets (AHA step 1 and 2) are shown in table one below.

Table One A comparison of the current American diet and American Heart Association guidelines.

Nutrient	Current US diet	Step 1 AHA diet	Step 2 AHA diet
Cholesterol	500 mg	< 300 mg	< 200 mg
Total Fat	~42%	< 30%	< 30%
Saturated Fat	~17%	<10%	< 7%
Carbohydrates		50-60%	50-60%
Protein		15-20%	15-20%

When dietary changes are followed for approximately six months, the maximum predicted reduction in cholesterol was 44 mg/dl for step 1 and 57 mg/dl for step two. These reductions are associated with a decrease in the risk for coronary artery disease but probably will not produce the desired lowering of cholesterol you are seeking, particularly if you are trying to get your cholesterol down to 150 mg/dl or less, which would place you in the lowest risk group for developing coronary artery disease. Of course, your cholesterol has to be taken into account with several other risk factors, as shown in appendix E at the end of this book, when determining your overall risk for heart disease.

NO STUDY HAS SHOWN THAT LOW CHOLESTEROL IS BAD

Beginning in the late 1980s, researchers began asking whether coronary artery disease could be reversed or at least limited by risk factor modification. In an attempt to answer this question, people were enrolled into programs designed to reduce their cholesterol levels. These studies used both dietary changes and drugs to reduce cholesterol and triglyceride levels. In 1990, we began investigating the importance of dietary changes and medication on reducing cholesterol and triglyceride levels.

> NO STUDY HAS SHOWN THAT HIGH
> CHOLESTEROL IS GOOD

By the summer of 1992, we began investigating the effect of diet versus drugs for the control of elevated cholesterol and triglyceride levels. Seventy people were enrolled in a study which was published in 1995 and was presented in London at the International Union of Angiology and at the American College of Cardiology Geriatrics Conference in New Orleans in 1995.

The seventy people were observed for 18 months to determine what happened to their cholesterol and triglyceride levels and to observe the amount of angina (chest pain from the heart) they had over time. Twenty-eight of the people (control) were seen by their doctor and were neither placed on a specific diet nor given medications to help with their cholesterol problem. The second group (diet) included 22 people who were encouraged to reduce as much fat and cholesterol from their diet as possible. No medications were given to these people, but they were seen frequently and received dietary counseling to help them further improve their eating habits. The third group (combination) of people consisted of seven people who received dietary counseling for the first six months of the study, but received medications for the entire 18 months. The remaining 13 people (medication) were given medications only and received no dietary guidance.

Over the next 18 months the people who received no medications and who continued their previous dietary patterns of eating had an average increase in their cholesterol levels of 15%. This represents a 30% increase in their risk for coronary artery disease on the basis of their cholesterol level alone. This increase can be seen in figure one, along with the results of the other groups.

PEOPLE WHO DIDN'T CHANGE THEIR DIETS
SHOWED AN AVERAGE INCREASE OF 15%
DURING THE 18 MONTH STUDY

The people who changed their diets to meet or exceed the changes outlined in the American Heart Association step 2 dietary recommendations, showed a 13% reduction in their cholesterol levels in six months and a 26% reduction in 18 months. This means that people with an average cholesterol level of 250 mg/dl at the beginning of the study were able to obtain cholesterol levels of 185 mg/dl or lower without the use of medications. Since then we have seen even greater reductions in cholesterol by placing people on fruit and vegetable diets and restricting their total calorie intake to allow them to lose one pound a week until they have reached ideal body weight.

PEOPLE WHO SIGNIFICANTLY REDUCED THEIR
CHOLESTEROL, FAT, AND CALORIE INTAKE SHOWED A
26% REDUCTION IN CHOLESTEROL DURING THE STUDY

When people made dietary changes and were given appropriate medications, there was a 37% reduction in cholesterol in as little as 6 months. The angina of many of these people ceased as did the need for drugs to treat angina. Some of this appears to be related to changes in the viscosity of the blood during the early stages of improvement. Further improvement seemed likely, but dietary counseling was discontinued and people returned to their old dietary habits. By the time another year had passed, these people had improved from where they started 18 months before but had actually lost ground during the last year of the study after they returned to their old diets, despite receiving appropriate medications to reduce their cholesterol. Overall their cholesterol levels decreased by 19% from the beginning to the end of the study. This is typical for what is seen when medications are used to treat elevated cholesterol levels, suggesting that many people using these medicines are not changing their poor dietary habits. The unfortunate part is that without continuing the improved diet, much of the benefit was lost.

WHEN PEOPLE DO NOT CHANGE THEIR DIETS, DRUGS CAN ONLY SLIGHTLY REDUCE CHOLESTEROL LEVELS

The final group of people received only medications and made no changes in their diet. These people had the same results the third group did by the end of the 18 months. It would appear that the appropriate use of medications may decrease your cholesterol levels by 13 to 19% over the course of a year and a half, but the potential benefit of these drugs is blunted because of the poor dietary habits of many individuals. Interestingly enough, this level of improvement is about the same after just 6 months of dietary (step 2 AHA) changes. If the diet is changed and medications are used even greater changes would be expected.

Figure One Changes in percent cholesterol in 18 months

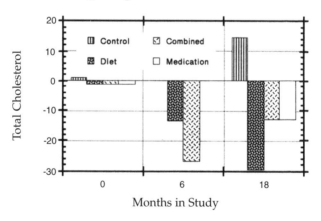

The results which were expected helped to answer many questions concerning the overall need for changing dieting habits if people expect to lower their cholesterol levels and keep them down. We have continued to look at the impact of further dietary modifications in an attempt to safely reduce cholesterol levels by diet alone. When a diet consisting primarily of fruits and vegetables is eaten, more impressive reductions in cholesterol and triglycerides, as well as weight (when appropriate), have been seen. As a result of increases in fiber from fruits, vegetables, and in some cases grains, there can be occasional problems with flatulence which can be easily handled with products like "Bean-O."

As we have seen, excessive calories of any type can result in increased production of triglycerides and cholesterol. The timing of meals as noted in chapter two is also important, since excessive evening calories frequently result in storage of calories instead of utilization. A purely fruit and vegetable diet is slightly more difficult than one which incorporates grain, breads, and pastas, but can be accomplished. Remember, protein is a necessary dietary component which is easily incorporated into a meatless diet. The use of multiple vitamins to prevent problems with vitamin deficiencies, such as vitamin B-12, can help to avoid problems. Whenever making dietary, exercise, or lifestyle changes it is important that you do so under the supervision of your doctor to determine if you have specific health needs that need to be addressed and to help you make progress without placing you at risk.

ALWAYS CONSULT YOUR DOCTOR WHEN PLANNING TO CHANGE YOUR DIET, EXERCISE LEVEL OR LIFESTYLE

One final point must be made regarding diet and cholesterol levels. Some people do not notice an immediate reduction in cholesterol and triglyceride (fat) levels despite following appropriate dietary changes. This may be because the cholesterol and fat we check for in the blood only represents seven percent of the body's total cholesterol as discussed earlier in chapter six. The remaining 93% is deposited throughout the body and may supply the body with the necessary building blocks to make more cholesterol and triglycerides, maintaining the elevated blood levels of fat and cholesterol. This is similar to a factory making cars. You can stop supplying raw materials to the factory, but if there are sufficient stores of parts and materials already in the warehouse, the factory can continue to make the cars until it runs out of parts. In the same way, if there is enough cholesterol and triglycerides (fat) stored in the body, you may quit feeding cholesterol, fat, and excess calories to the body, but the liver is still able to make cholesterol and triglycerides, until the stores are sufficiently depleted. Since we have no practical way of determining how much cholesterol and fat is stored in any given individual, it becomes a matter of persistence to find out when these stores of cholesterol and fats will be sufficiently depleted to allow blood levels of cholesterol and triglycerides to return to safer levels.

In the next several chapters we will review the nutritional contents of many foods and meals which can be made from these foods. These, in addition to your doctor's help, will hopefully allow you to reduce your cholesterol and triglyceride levels, along with your weight if appropriate. Bon appetite!

Food Section

In this chapter we will look at five basic food groups: 1) fruits, 2) vegetables, 3) milk and dairy products, 4) grains, cereals, and pasta, and 5) meats. Each section will have foods listed alphabetically so you can easily find them and determine how many calories are present in a serving size as listed in the tables. You will also find the grams of fat, saturated fat, carbohydrates, approximate protein, and milligrams of cholesterol for each serving listed. When beginning to prepare healthier meals it is also important that you follow the serving size or at least take it into account; if the serving you have is greater than that shown, you **will** be eating more calories, fat, etc.

FRUIT

Food item	Amount of food	Calories	Fat Grams	Sat. Fat grams	Carbo. grams	Protein grams	Chol. (mgs.)
Apple	one med	80	0.6	0.1	21.1	0	0
Applesauce	1/4 cup	50	0.1	0	12.7	0	0
Apricot	one med	17	0	0	4	0	0
Banana	one med	105	0.5	0.2	26.7	0	0
Blackberries	1/4 cup	24	0.2	0.1	5.9	0	0

How to Bypass Your Bypass

Food item	Amount of food	Calories	Fat Grams	Sat. Fat grams	Carbo. grams	Protein grams	Chol. (mgs.)
Blueberries	1/4 cup	20	0.2	0	4.7	0	0
Boysenberries	1/2 cup	33	0.2	0	7.8	0	0
Breadfruit (5″ diameter)	1/2	94	0.7	0	21.9	0	0
Cantaloupe (5″ diameter)	1/4	47	0.5	0.1	11	0	0
Casabas	1/2 cup	23	0.1	0	5.5	0	0
Cherries	10 med	49	0.7	0.1	10.5	0	0
Crabapples	1/2 cup	42	0.2	0.1	9.8	0	0
Cranberries	1/2 cup	27	0.1	0	6.5	0	0
Currants	1/2 cup	31	0.1	0	7.5	0	0
Dates	1/4 cup	122	0.2	0.1	32.7	0	0
Figs	1/4 cup	121	1.7	0.7	26.6	0	0
Fruit Cocktail (in water)	1/2 cup	40	0.1	0	9.8	0	0
Gooseberries	1/2 cup	34	0.9	0.1	6.2	0	0
Grapefruit (3-3/4″ diameter)	1/2	38	0.1	0	9.3	0	0
Grapes (Thompson)	10	35	0	0	9	0	0
Guava	one med	45	0.5	0.2	9.7	0	0
Honeydew melon 6 1/2″ diameter	1/10	45	0	0	12	0	0
Kiwi	one med	46	0	0	11	0	0
Kumquats	one med	12	0	0	3	0	0
Lemon	one med	17	0.2	0	3.8	0	0
Lime	one med	20	0.1	0	4.8	0	0
Loganberries	1/2 cup	40	0.2	0	9.6	0	0
Loquats	one med	5	0	0	1.2	0	0
Lychees	one med	6	0	0	1.5	0	0
Mangos	one med	135	1	0.1	35	0	0
Mulberries	1/2 cup	31	0.6	0	6.4	0	0
Nectarines	one med	67	0.6	0	15.4	0	0
Orange	one med	60	0.2	0	15.4	0	0
Papayas	1/2 cup	27	0.1	0.1	4.9	0	0

Food item	Amount of food	Calories	Fat Grams	Sat. Fat grams	Carbo. grams	Protein grams	Chol. (mgs.)
Passion Fruit	one med	18	0.1	0	4.3	0	0
Peach	one med	37	0	0	9.2	0	0
Pear	one med	100	0.7	0	25.1	0	0
Persimmon (native)	one med	32	0.1	0	7.8	0	0
Persimmon (Japanese)	one med	118	0.3	0	28.8	0	0
Pineapple	1/2 cup	39	0.3	0.1	8.9	0	0
Plantains	one med	218	0.7	0	52.9	0	0
Plums	one med	36	0.4	4	8.1	0	0
Pomegranates	one med	104	0.5	0	24.9	0	0
Prickly pear	one med	42	0.5	0	9.4	0	0
Prunes	1/4 cup	60	0.1	0	14.9	0	0
Pummelo	one med	228	0.2	0	59.6	0	0
Quice	one med	53	0.2	0.1	12.6	0	0
Raisins	1/4 cup	110	0.2	0.1	28.7	0	0
Raspberries	1/2 cup	31	0.3	0	7.1	0	0
Rhubarb	1/2 cup	14	0	0	3.5	0	0
Strawberries	1/4 cup	11	0.3	0	2.8	0	0
Tamarinds	one med	5	0	0	1.2	0	0
Tangerines	one med	37	0.2	0	8.8	0	0
Watermelon	1/2 cup	25	0.3	0	5.6	0	0

One of the frequent problems people have when changing their diets, is becoming familiar with foods which are different from what they normally eat. There are a variety of fruits, prepared and packaged in several ways, which are not shown here. Several books are available which list all the different brand name foods available as well as their ingredients. The same information can be obtained from food labels found on packaged food items. The more than 50 different types of fruits listed above show that there is a large variety of fruits available to choose from. Undoubtedly, you noticed the two varieties of persimmons, native and Japanese, in the table above. It is important that you pay attention to the types of foods you select if you are going to accurately determine the caloric and nutritional values of them. If you picked a Japanese persimmon, while good tasting, you'll get almost four times the number of calories present in the native variety.

In general, fruits are not only good sources of carbohydrates, but are relatively low in fats, saturated fats, and tend to be free of cholesterol. Additionally, they are good sources of dietary fiber as well as antioxidant vitamins. In the next section, we will focus on vegetables which, with only a few exceptions, have the same desirable qualities as the fruits.

FRUITS MAKE EXCELLENT SNACKS, DESSERTS, AND SIDE DISHES

VEGETABLES

Food item	Amount of food	Calories	Fat Grams	Sat. Fat grams	Carbo. grams	Protein grams	Chol. (mgs.)
Alfalfa sprouts	1/4 cup	2.5	0	0	0.3	0.3	0
Artichoke	one med	65	0.3	0.1	15.6	0	0
Asparagus	1/4 cup	11.5	0	0	2	0.9	0
Bamboo shoots	1/4 cup	6.3	0.3	0	1	0	0
Bean sprouts	1 cup	11	0	0	2.7	0	0
Beans, baked	1/2 cup	151	1	0	34	1.5	0
Beans, garbanzo	1/2 cup	143	1.4	0.1	32.6	-	0
Beans, green	1/4 cup	11	0	0	2.5	0.2	0
Beans, fava	1/2 cup	90	< 1	0	20	0	< 1
Beans, lima	1/4 cup	65	0.3	0.1	12.2	3.4	0
Beans, red kidney	1/4 cup	55	0.2	0	9.9	3.4	0
Beans, refried	1/4 cup	104	4	1.6	11	6	6
Beans, vegetarian	1/4 cup	60	0.3	0	13.1	1.2	0
Beans, navy	1/4 cup	60	0.3	0	13.1	1.2	0
Beets (pickled)	1/4 cup	37	0	0	9.5	0	0
Beet greens	1/2 cup	20	0.1	0	4.7	0	0

Food item	Amount of food	Calories	Fat Grams	Sat. Fat grams	Carbo. grams	Protein grams	Chol. (mgs.)
Broccoli	1/4 cup	6	0.05	0	1.3	0	0
Brussel sprouts	1/4 cup	16.3	0.3	0	3.3	0.1	0
Cabbage	1/4 cup	4	0	0	1	0	0
Carrots	1/4 cup	12	0.05	0	3	0	0
Cauliflower	1/4 cup	6	0	0	1	0.5	0
Celery	1/4 cup	5.5	0	0	1	0.4	0
Chayote (1" piece)	1/2 cup	16	0.2	0	3.5	0	0
Chives	one tbs.	1	0	0	0.2	0	0
Cilantro	1/4 cup	1	0.1	0	0	0	0
Corn	1/4 cup	34	0.05	0	8.4	0	0
Corn, sweet	1/2 cup	89	1.1	0.2	19.8	0	0
Cowpeas	1/2 cup	89	0.7	0.2	20.7	0	0
Cucumbers (1/4" slices)	3	4	0.1	0	1	0	0
Dandelion greens	1/2 cup	17	0.3	0	3.5	0	0
Dill weed	5 sprigs	0	0	0	0	0	0
Eggplant	one med	27	0.1	0	6.5	0	0
Endive	1/2 cup	4	0.1	0	0.7	0	0
Garlic	1 clove	4	0	0	1	0	0
Ginger root (1/8 by 1")	5 peices	8	0.1	0	1.7	0	0
Jicama slices	1 cup	46	0.1	0	11.2	0	0
Kale	1/2 cup	17	0.2	0	3.8	0	0
Kohlrabi slices	1/2 cup	19	0.1	0	4.5	0	0
Lentils	1/4 cup	55	0	0	9.6	4.2	0
Leeks	1/4 cup	16	0.1	0	3.7	0	0
Lettuce, iceberg	1/4 cup	1.8	0	0	0.3	0.15	0
Mixed vegetables*	1/4 cup	25	0.1	0	5.6	0.4	0
Mushrooms	1/4 cup	9.5	0	0	2	0.4	0
Mustard greens	1/2 cup	11	0.2	0	2.3	0	0

*carrots, corn, and peas

How to Bypass Your Bypass

Food item	Amount of food	Calories	Fat Grams	Sat. Fat grams	Carbo. grams	Protein grams	Chol. (mgs.)
Okra slices	1/2 cup	19	0.1	0	4.5	0	0
Onions	1/4 cup	15.3	0	0	3.5	0.3	0
Parsley	1/2 cup	11	0.2	0	2.3	0	0
Parsnips	1/2 cup	50	0.4	0	11.6	0	0
Peas, black-eyed	1/4 cup	50	0.2	0.1	8.6	3.4	0
Peas, green	1/2 cup	63	0.3	0.1	15	0	0
Peppers, chili	one med	18	0.1	0	4.2	0	0
Peppers, sweet red	1 ounce	5	0	0	1.2	0	0
Peppers, sweet yellow	1 large	50	0.4	0	11.6	0	0
Pinto beans	1/2 cup	117	0.4	0.1	28.4	0	0
Pumpkin	1/2 cup	24	0.9	0.1	3.9	0	0
Radicchio	1/2 cup	5	0.1	0	1	0	0
Rutabagas	1/2 cup	25	0.1	0	6	0	0
Shallots	one tbs.	7	0	0	1.7	0	0
Snow Peas	1/2 cup	30	0.1	0	7.2	0	0
Taro	1/2 cup	56	0.1	0	13.7	0	0
Tomatillos	one med	11	0.4	0	1.8	0	0
Tomatoes, green	one med	30	0.3	0	6.8	0	0
Tomatoes, red	1/2 cup	24	0.3	0	5.3	0	0
Turnips	1/2 cup	14	0.1	0	3.2	0	0
Turnip greens	1/2 cup	7	0.1	0	1.5	0	0
Watercress	1/2 cup	2	0	0	0.5	0	0
Yams	1/2 cup	79	0.1	0	19.5	0	0
Zucchini	1/2 cup	14	0.1	0	3.2	0	0

Like the fruit section, the vegetables listed above are for the most part fresh. Packaging can change foods and the actual ingredients are listed on the food labels of processed and packaged foods. Fresh food, however, doesn't come with a label and the above tables will help you decide how nutritious the foods are that you're eating. Additionally, if you modify a recipe, using the tables in this chapter will allow you to determine what you've done by adding or removing something from a recipe. Almost any food can be fried, coated, or have a sauce added which adds calories, fat, and cholesterol to the picture.

Because of the high fat content, foods like avocados and olives are frequently listed with oils. In 3 tablespoons of pureed avocado there are 76 calories, with 7.5 grams of total fat, 1.1 grams of saturated fat and no cholesterol. Five green olives have 17 calories, but 1.8 grams of total fat, 0.2 grams of which is saturated. Black olives by comparison have 15 calories with 1.6 grams of fat including 0.2 grams of saturated fat. There is no cholesterol in either green or ripe olives. While the overall number of calories does not appear to be impressive, avocados are 88.8 percent fat, while green and black olives are 95.3 and 96 percent fat respectively.

In table three of chapter one, hypothyroidism was listed as a cause of hypercholesterolemia. Cabbage, rutabagas, and turnips contain chemicals known as "thioglycoside precursors." These chemicals can cause goiter and hypothyroidism if eaten in large enough quantities. Some of my patients who are originally from the oriental region of the world have eaten large enough quantities of these foods (particularly cabbage) to have high cholesterol levels. For them, treatment of their high cholesterol must focus on reducing the amount of these foods in their diet as well as other dietary changes. Clearly, you are what you eat.

Milk and Dairy Products

In this category we will look at three different groups 1) cheese, 2) milk, and 3) other.

CHEESES

Food item	Amount of food	Calories	Fat Grams	Sat. Fat grams	Carbo. grams	Protein grams	Chol. (mgs.)
American	1 oz	105	8.9	5.6	0.4	5.8	27
Cheddar	1 oz	115	9.4	6	0.4	7.2	30
Mozzarella - part skim milk	1 oz	70	4.5	3.1	0.8	6.5	16
Mozzarella - whole	1 oz	80	6	3.7	1	5.5	22
Parmesan	1 oz	129	9	5.4	1	11	22
Provolone	1 oz	100	8	4.8	1	6	20
Ricotta - part skim milk	1/4 cup	85	4.8	3	3.3	7.1	19
Ricotta - whole milk	1/4 cup	107	8	5	1.8	6.9	31
Swiss	1 oz	107	8	5	1	7.7	26

Unlike ten to twenty years ago, there are now a wide variety of cheeses available which are made from low-fat milk or even better skim milk. There are also a number of low sodium (salt) cheeses which are important for many people with heart problems or high blood pressure. While there are many cheeses available which are not listed here, the examples above illustrate several important points. Part-skim milk mozzarella cheese is the lowest calorie and cholesterol cheese typically seen in the grocery store/supermarket. Before you decide that this means it's low in fat, please remember that for each gram of fat there are nine calories.

For each one ounce slice of part-skim mozzarella cheese there are 40.5 calories from fat.

40.5 fat calories = (4.5 grams of fat) (9 calories/gram of fat)

This means that almost 58% of the total calories come from fat.

57.8% calories from fat = 40.5 fat calories/70 total calories

MILK

Food item	Amount of food	Calories	Fat Grams	Sat. Fat grams	Carbo. grams	Protein grams	Chol. (mgs.)
Skim	8 oz	86	0.4	0.3	11.9	8.7	4
One Percent	8 oz	102	2.5	1.6	11.7	8.2	10
Two Percent	8 oz	121	4.8	2.9	11.7	7.8	22
Whole (~3.2%)	8 oz	150	8.2	5.1	11.4	7.6	33
1% chocolate	8 oz	160	2.5	1.5	26.1	8.3	7
2% chocolate	8 oz	180	5	3.1	26	7.8	17
Buttermilk	8 oz	99	2	1.3	12	8.2	9
Condensed sweetened milk	8 oz	982	27	1.7	166	18.7	104
Non-fat dry milk	8 oz	90	0.2	0	12.9	9.2	5

While many people consider milk to be a good source of protein, as the percentage of fat increases from skim to whole milk, the protein decreases from 8.7 grams to 7.6 grams per eight ounce serving. We also see an increase in cholesterol, total fat, and saturated fat. Clearly you get to make a choice about whether you want protein or fat and cholesterol. Even skim milk is not without some fat as shown in the table below.

Percent of Calories from Fat

Type of Milk	Percent of Calories from Fat
Skim	4.2%
One Percent	22%
Two Percent	35.7%
Whole Mile (~3.2%)	49.2%

OTHER DAIRY PRODUCTS

Food item	Amount of food	Calories	Fat Grams	Sat. Fat grams	Carbo. grams	Protein grams	Chol. (mgs.)
Butter	1 tsp.	35	3.8	2.5	0	0	10
Egg	one lrg.	70	4.5	1.5	< 1.0	6	215
Margarine - 80% fat (hard)	1 tsp.	36	4	0.8	0	0	0
Yogurt - skim milk	1 cup	110	0	0	18	9	< 5
Yogurt - 2% milk	1 cup	250	4	3	45	9	15

In the past decade there has been much confusion regarding the difference between butter and margarine. In reality, the issue was moot, both butter and margarine are high in fat, with butter having slightly more saturated fat and cholesterol than margarine. The difference between the two is like asking whether you would prefer to be shot with a .38 caliber or .45 caliber bullet. Most intelligent people would prefer not to be shot.

NEITHER BUTTER NOR MARGARINE ARE HEART HEALTHY

This type of back and forth adjusting of numbers reminds me of the coffee controversy which has been generated over the last several years. What we now know is that five to ten cups of caffenated coffee per day will tend to increase your cholesterol level. The amount of increase is not entirely clear.

We will now look at grains to determine their nutritional content. This is a particularly problematic area since most grains are actually good for you and provide minerals and vitamins in your diet. The problem becomes one of hidden fat and the overall number of calories you eat as a result of eating breads, cereals, and pasta. Crackers, which are not listed in the table, can be assumed to be relatively high in fat (chapter five) content unless the package label proves otherwise. Highly processed foods with hydrogenated fats added are clearly not heart healthy. As we learned in chapter two, if you eat more calories than your body needs, it will make fats and cholesterol whether the food you are eating is relatively good for you or not. For this reason I advise my patients to limit the amounts of grains they eat as well as the time of day they are eating.

GRAINS, CERELS, AND PASTA

Food item	Amount of food	Calories	Fat Grams	Sat. Fat grams	Carbo. grams	Protein grams	Chol. (mgs.)
Bagel	one	200	1.8	0.3	38.2	7.7	0
Baking Powder Bisquit	one	164	7	1.7	22	3.2	0
BREADS							
Hamburger bun (whole wheat)	one	174	4	0	30	4.5	0
Italian Bread	one slice	143	1	0.3	28	5.5	0
Pita Bread	one	165	0.9	0.1	33	6.2	0
Pumpernickel	one slice	80	1	0.2	15	2.7	0
Rye Bread	one slice	65	0.9	0.2	12	2.2	0
White Bread	one slice	65	1	0.3	12.2	1.8	0
Whole Wheat	one slice	70	1.2	0.3	12.5	2.3	0
PASTAS							
Acini De Pepe	1/3 cup	210	1	0	42	7	0
Bow Ties	1 cup	210	1	0	43	7	0
Capellini	2 oz	210	1	0	40	9	0
Dumpling noodles	2 oz	210	1	0	40	9	0
Egg Bow Ties	1 cup	220	3	1	40	7	55
Egg noodles	2 oz	210	2.5	1	38	10	70
Elbow macaroni	2 oz	210	1	0	40	9	0
Fettuccini	2 oz	210	2.5	1	38	10	45
Fideo mediano	2 oz	210	1	0	40	9	0

How to Bypass Your Bypass

Food item	Amount of food	Calories	Fat Grams	Sat. Fat grams	Carbo. grams	Protein grams	Chol. (mgs.)
Jumbo shells	5 pieces	200	1	0	38	6	0
Kluski egg noodles	1 cup	220	3	1	40	8	55
Lasagna	2 oz	210	1	0	40	9	0
Linguini	2 oz	210	1	0	40	9	0
Manicotti	2 oz	210	1	0	40	9	0
Mostaccioli	2 oz	210	1	0	40	9	0
Penne rigate	1/2 cup	210	1	0	42	7	0
Ribbons (yolk free)	2 oz	200	1	0	40	8	0
Rigatoni	2 oz	210	1	0	42	7	0
Rotini	2 oz	210	1	0	40	9	0
Shell macaroni	2 oz	210	1	0	42	7	0
Spaghetti	2 oz	210	1	0	42	7	0
Spinach egg noodles	1 - 1/4 cups	220	3	1	40	8	55
Tortellini with parmesan cheese	1/2 cup	210	4	3	36	10	40
Vermicelli	2 oz	210	1	0	40	9	0
Whole wheat noodles	2 oz	190	2	1	34	10	30
Ziti	3/4 cup	210	1	0	42	7	0
RICE							
Barley	1/4 cup	170	1	0	37	5	0
Brown rice	1/2 cup	170	1.5	0.5	34	4	0
California brown rice	1/4 cup	160	1.5	0	34	3	0
Calrose rice	1/4 cup	170	0.5	0	38	3	0
Converted rice	1/4 cup	170	0	0	38	4	0
Couscous	1/3 cup	220	1	0	46	8	0
Cracked wheat	1/4 cup	150	0.5	0	32	4	0
Falafel	1/4 cup	100	1	0	18	10	0
Lentil pilaf	2 oz	170	0.5	0	37	10	0
Long grain rice	1/4 cup	150	0	0	35	3	0
Rice pilaf	2 oz	190	0.5	0	42	6	0

Food item	Amount of food	Calories	Fat Grams	Sat. Fat grams	Carbo. grams	Protein grams	Chol. (mgs.)
Spanish rice	2.5 oz	230	1	0	52	6	0
Taboule mix	1 oz	90	0	0	20	3	0
Wheat pilaf	2 oz	180	0.5	0	42	6	0
White rice	1/2 cup	170	0	0	37	4	0
White and wild rice mix	1/4 cup	170	0.5	0	36	4	0
Yellow rice	1/3 cup	190	0	0	43	5	0

Breads, crackers, and other processed foods have higher levels of fat and saturated fat than fruits and vegetables. You can now find specifically prepared breads and crackers with reduced fat contents. This is something which should be apparent from the food label. As we discovered in chapter five, reduced fat doesn't mean no fat. These changes in processed foods are the direct result of consumer concerns over the calories and fats in their food. Many of the pastas, rices, and legumes are excellent sources of both carbohydrates and protein, which explains their ability to be used in the place of meats as protein sources. Additionally, the iron content of many pastas exceed that found in some meats. So much for the myth that you need meat to obtain your iron. In fact, some breakfast cereals are well fortified sources of iron.

REDUCED FAT DOESN'T MEAN NO FAT

It is also important to remember that the calories, fats, carbohydrates, and cholesterol noted above and for any of the foods in this chapter does not take into account the added calories, fats, carbohydrates, and cholesterol that you add by using sauces, gravies, condiments, or anything else.

Finally, we are going to look at several types of meats. Many of the beef products available today only list the percent meat; for example 90% fat free. Obviously, one is left to conclude that 10% of the meat is fat. Looking at what we learned from the food labels in chapter five and what we have learned in this chapter when comparing skim milk with one percent, two percent, and whole milk, knowing the percent fat doesn't tell you what the percentage of calories are from fat. Hopefully, changes in food labeling requirements for the different meats will soon occur so consumers can compare different types and cuts of meat.

TYPICALLY 97% FAT FREE MEANS ABOUT 30%
OF THE CALORIES ARE FROM FAT

MEATS

Food item	Amount of food	Calories	Fat Grams	Sat. Fat grams	Carbo. grams	Protein grams	Chol. (mgs.)
Bacon	3 slices	80	7	2.5	1	5	10
Beef (lean pressed)	2.5 oz	120	7	3	1	13	40
Bologna	1 slice	120	11	5	2	4	30
Braunsch- weiger	2 oz	180	16	6	2	7	80
Buffalo wings	3 pieces	160	12	2.5	0	14	90
Burritos (bean and cheese)	one	240	6	1.5	38	8	5
Canadian bacon	2 oz	60	1.5	0	1	10	30
Corn dogs	one	220	12	3	23	6	15
Corned beef brisket	4 oz	200	14	6	< 1	17	60
CHICKEN							
Breast (skinless)	one	140	1.5	0	0	29	75
Drumstick	two	230	12	3	0	27	115
Fried patties	one	330	23	5	18	15	40
Leg quarter	4 oz	270	20	6	0	19	90
Pressed (lean)	2.5 oz	120	7	2	1	14	65
Tenderloin	4 oz	130	1.5	0	0	27	65
Wings	three	280	20	6	0	23	95
FRANKS							
Beef	one	190	17	7	2	6	35
Turkey	one	70	6	1.5	0	4	30
97% fat free	one	50	1.5	0.5	4	6	20

Considerable debate has occurred about whether chicken or fish is better for you than beef. Studies now show that it's not the type of meat that you eat, but the amount of cholesterol and fats present. Cholesterol from chickens has the same effect as cholesterol from beef, ham, or anything else.

MEATS

Food item	Amount of food	Calories	Fat Grams	Sat. Fat grams	Carbo. grams	Protein grams	Chol. (mgs.)
HAM							
Ham	3 oz	120	8	3	1	13	45
Picnic	3 oz	170	13	3	1	11	40
Pressed (lean)	2.5 oz	120	7	2.5	1	12	40
Shank (skinless)	3 oz	130	8	3	2	13	50
Steaks (97% fat free)	one slice	60	2	0.5	0	10	30

Ham is an interesting meat in that there is frequently large amounts of sodium (salt) present. For example, the shank has 1,240 milligrams of sodium for every three ounce serving. Earlier we mentioned concerns about the labeling of meats, such as beef. The example of ham steak in the above table is a good example to use to better understand this. For every slice there are two grams of total fat, which means that there are 18 fat calories in the one piece.

18 fat calories = (2 grams of fat)(9 calories/gram of fat)

This means that for a ham steak which is 97% fat free, that 30% of the calories come from fat.

$$30\% = \frac{18 \text{ fat calories}}{60 \text{ total calories}}$$

Remember, it's not the type of meat but the fat and cholesterol content that you need to be watching out for.

CHOLESTEROL IS CHOLESTEROL REGARDLESS OF WHERE IT COMES FROM

MEATS

Food item	Amount of food	Calories	Fat Grams	Sat. Fat grams	Carbo. grams	Protein grams	Chol. (mgs.)
Herring (wine sauce	2 oz	120	5	1.5	10	9	30
Imitation crab	1/2 cup	80	0	0	10	9	10
Italian meatballs	six	250	18	7	5	15	40
LAMB							
Chop loin	3 oz	250	18	7	0	22	85
Leg	3 oz	210	12	5		22	80
Shank	3 oz	210	11	5	3.7	24	90
Shoulder	3 oz	230	15	7	2.7	21	80
Whole	3 oz	210	12	5		22	80

Some lamb are genetically different in that they are leaner with less obvious fat. This is typical of some of the breeds present in the United Kingdom.

MEATS

Food item	Amount of food	Calories	Fat Grams	Sat. Fat grams	Carbo. grams	Protein grams	Chol. (mgs.)
Pastrami	2.5 oz	100	5	2	< 1	14	50
Pepperoni	1 oz	140	13	6	0	5	35
PORK							
Belly (salt)	2 oz	300	31	11	0	4	30
Ground	3 oz	250	18	7	0	22	80
Ribs	three	350	23	9	17	20	50
Sirloin	3 oz	220	14	5	0	23	75
Tenderloin	3 oz	150	5	2	2.2	24	65
Salami	2 slices	90	7	3	1	6	35
Salmon (smoked)	3 oz	80	1.5	0	1	16	35
Sandwich spread	2 oz	140	10	3.5	8	4	25

Food item	Amount of food	Calories	Fat Grams	Sat. Fat grams	Carbo. grams	Protein grams	Chol. (mgs.)
Sausage - party	6 links	170	16	6	1	7	35
Sausage - polish	2 oz	190	17	8	2	7	25
Sausage - summer	2 oz	190	16	8	<1	9	30
Sausage - turkey	1 link	170	10	3	0	19	90
Turkey - pressed (lean)	2.5 oz	120	7	2	1	12	55
Turkey - 97% fat free	1 slice	30	1	0.5	1	5	10
Veal patties (breaded)	one	340	21	6	20	16	45

Wild game typically has less fat than domesticated animals. This is a result of differences in types of foods available for wild animals and the sedentary lifestyles of domesticated animals. It would appear, that like people, if animals are feed a lot of calories and are not very active, they become heavier with more cholesterol. Fortunately, domesticated animals are sacrificed before they can develop heart disease. This is probably good since I know of no surgeon trained to performing coronary artery bypass operations on a cow.

The amount of protein in different foods is typically not listed in food tables, leading people to wonder about sources of protein. Most people assume that to get the amount of protein needed in a day, they must eat meat. This is clearly not the case as we have seen in the above tables. Foods such as legumes, seeds, nuts, and grains are considered to be complementary (figure one) sources of protein and can be combined to provide adequate amounts of protein in the diet.

How to Bypass Your Bypass

Figure One Complementary protein sources

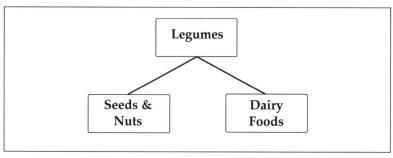

In the next section we will look at some recipe ideas for healthier meals primarily using fruits, vegetables, and some grains, cereals, and pastas.

Menus

B efore beginning the specific recipes, there are several cooking or preparation hints which can help reduce the fat and cholesterol in your diet using your current recipes.

Hints to Reducing Fat and Cholesterol in Your Current Recipes

1) Oil is used to conduct heat during the cooking process. Water can be used in the place of oil, but requires that you add smaller quantities of water more frequently than you do oil.

2) After meat has been cooked, oils, fats, and cholesterol are present in the juice/broth. This can be eliminated from your diet by pouring off the juice.

3) Foods should be baked or steamed, never fried. Frying only adds additional fat.

4) Poultry should always have the skin removed to reduce fat and cholesterol.

5) Applesauce can be used in place of some of the oils in breads.

6) Use fresh or frozen fruits and vegetables whenever possible. Canned foods have salt added to help preserve them.

7) Yogurt can frequently be used in the place of mayonnaise.

8) When learning what a serving size is, you need to practice measuring servings of food. For example, 2 ounces of something is a weight not an eyeball estimate.

9) Slow down while eating. The longer you take to eat your food, the longer it will last and the more satisfied you are likely to be.

10) Water is a necessary part of life and most people agree that you need about 8 glasses (8-12 ounces) a day. Water has no calories.

11) Dieting is something you do for a short time. Changing your diet is something you do for a lifetime.

12) All meat has protein, not all protein is meat.

13) Ketchup and salt are not the only condiments available. Foods can be seasoned without adding salt or fat by using basil, parsley, pepper, mustard, and a whole host of other seasonings to enhance the flavor of your food.

14) Salad isn't just lettuce leaves. The more colorful and varied a salad, the more enjoyable it is.

15) Lemon juice can be added to cut fruits to prevent browning while waiting to be served. It also gives added tartness.

16) Lemon juice makes an excellent salad dressing.

17) Never cook your vegetables in water. Either steam them, stir fry them, or eat them raw. Vegetables cooked in water loose vitamins and minerals when the water is poured off. Additionally, vegetables taste better when crisp than when limp.

18) You can usually substitute egg beaters for eggs in recipes, or two egg whites for each whole egg to reduce your cholesterol intake.

19) When eating out or taking airplane trips, ask about special diets which reduce fats, cholesterol, and calories. Most airlines have special vegetarian meals, including western and eastern versions.

20) Chilled fruits make excellent desserts.

Making Your Own Hot Salsa

Many recipes use salsa or spicy condiments to add flavor. Here is an example of one which can be adjusted to your own taste for salads, dips, et cetera.

Combine the following: two medium chopped tomatoes, one medium onion, 2 tablespoons chopped cilantro, and 3 cloves of minced garlic. To this add jalapeños which have had the seeds and stems removed. When removing the seeds, wear gloves to prevent problems with burning or injury to your skin. Do not touch your face or any other part of your body without thoroughly cleaning your hands. The jalapeños can be added to the rest of the salsa. One tablespoon of lemon juice can also be added. If you want to make this spicier, add more jalapeño, garlic, or cilantro. If you want it less spicy, reduce the jalapeño, garlic, cilantro, or add tomatoes (or perhaps both).

Preparing Dried Beans for Recipes

All beans which are bought should be spread out and examined, removing any which are damaged. Place the beans in cold water and remove any which float. Leave the remaining beans in the cold water and allow to soak for 8 to 12 hours, preferably overnight. You do not need to soak lentils or split peas. Drain the beans and return to a saucepan and cover with about an inch of water. Bring the beans to a simmer and skim off any foam on the surface. Boil for about 10 minutes and then follow the cooking instructions for your individual recipe.

Menu Section

As with each of the menus listed, you can easily vary the ingredients to create new and interesting recipes of your own. You can determine the nutritional values of foods you add and remove from your new recipe by using chapter nine or looking at food labels. Recipes are an interesting thing. My great-grandparents started a restaurant in the 1930s to 40s in the mid-west, and like many other restaurants, these recipes were and still are highly guarded. The recipes that follow have been around in one form or another for some time. Each one probably has some variation of one you might have seen or had but didn't think about using. People who are highly creative can have a lot of fun making nutritious meals.

APPLES ON A CLOUD

Ingredients

4 medium yellow delicious apples
1 teaspoon vanilla or almond flavoring
1/2 cup water
1/2 teaspoon finely shredded lemon peel
1 tablespoon lemon juice
3 sticks cinnamon
1/2 cup egg substitute
3 tablespoons sugar

Peel, core, and thinly slice the apples. In a medium saucepan combine the water, lemon juice, and cinnamon sticks. Bring to a boil. Add the apples and return to boiling. Reduce the heat and simmer for about 8 to 10 minutes until the apples are tender. Stir occasionally. Once the apples are tender, remove from the heat and add the vanilla or almond flavoring. Remove the cinnamon sticks and let stand for 15 minutes.

In a small mixing bowl beat the egg substitute until soft peaks occur. Slowly add one tablespoon of the liquid from the apples, the lemon peel, and the sugar. Mix at a high speed until stiff peaks form.

Preheat your oven to 325° F.

Evenly divide the apple slices and juice into six six-ounce custard cups and cover with the egg substitute mixture. Place the custard cups in the oven for about 10 minutes or until the egg mixture becomes a light brown. Serve warm.

Approximate Nutritional Values:

Serving size: 1/6 recipe
Calories: 128 calories
Fat: 0 grams
Carbohydrates: 30 grams
Protein: 2 grams
Cholesterol: 0 milligrams

APPLE SALAD

Ingredients

2 cups chopped red delicious apples
1 20 ounce can chunk pineapple, drain off juice and reserve
1/4 cup raisins
1/2 cup sliced celery
1 tablespoon raw cashews
1/3 cup nonfat plain or vanilla flavored yogurt

Combine the apples, pineapple, raisins, celery, and cashews in a mixing bowl. Whisk together one-third cup nonfat yogurt with one-half cup reserved pineapple juice. The yogurt-pineapple juice combination should be poured over the fruit mixture and thoroughly mixed. Chill for at least 30 minutes prior to serving.

Approximate Nutritional Values:

Serving size: 1/6 recipe
Calories: 130 calories
Fat: 0.5 grams
Carbohydrates: 29 grams
Protein: 2 grams
Cholesterol: 0.5 milligrams

APPLES AND CABBAGE

Ingredients

2 tablespoons water
2 tablespoons apple juice

1 large Jonathan or Rome Beauty apple cut into thin slices
3 cups cabbage (usually red)
1/2 medium onion cut in then slices

1/2 teaspoon chicken bouillon
1 tablespoon red wine vinegar

Place two tablespoons of apple juice and two tablespoons of water to a large saucepan. Then, mix in one large apple, 1/2 medium sized onion and approximately three cups of shredded cabbage. Add 1/2 tsp. of chicken bouillon. Bring the mixture to a boil, cover, and simmer (by reducing heat) for about five minutes until the apples and cabbage are tender. Add 1 tbs. of red wine vinegar. Serve without juice.

Approximate Nutritional Values:

Serving size: 1/4 recipe
Calories: 60 calories
Fat: 0 grams
Carbohydrates: 14 grams
Protein: 1 gram
Cholesterol: 0 milligrams

ASPARAGUS SALAD

Ingredients

4 cups fresh asparagus
4 cups fresh mushrooms
8-9 cups fresh lettuce (any variety)

Rinse and clean 4 cups of fresh asparagus, 4 cups of fresh mushrooms, and 8 to 9 cups of fresh lettuce. Varying the variety of lettuce allows a variety of different salads without changing the nutritional content of the salad. This should be mixed and placed in your refrigerator overnight if possible. This salad is excellent without any salad dressing, but if you must, there are several low fat, no cholesterol salad dressings available on the market today.

Approximate Nutritional Values:

Serving size: 1/3 cup
Calories: 40 calories
Fat: < 1 gram
Carbohydrates: 7 grams
Protein: 3 grams
Cholesterol: 0 milligrams

ASPARAGUS AND MUSHROOMS

Ingredients

1 pound asparagus
2 cups sliced mushrooms
1/2 cup chopped red tomato

Spray a nonstick cooking spray on a skillet and add one pound of chopped asparagus. After 4 to 5 minutes add 2 cups of sliced mushrooms and continue to stir the mixture for 2 more minutes. Add 1/2 cup of red tomato and stir for 30 to 60 seconds.

Approximate Nutritional Values:

Serving size: 1/4 recipe
Calories: 36 calories
Fat: 1 gram
Carbohydrates: 6 grams
Protein: 3 grams
Cholesterol: 0 milligrams

A nice addition to this recipe includes a few nuts, pumpkin seeds, or sunflower seeds. If you add these be prepared to increase the calorie and fat content of each serving.

BANANA MIX

Ingredients

1 large Jonathan, Rome Beauty, or Winesap apple
1 large ripe banana
1 medium nectarine
3/4 cup pineapple

2 tablespoons lime or lemon juice to taste

Slice the banana and the apple. The pineapple should be cubed. The nectarine is pitted and cubed. All four fruits are then added together and mixed with lemon or lime juice to prevent discoloration. This is best if the fruit is chilled before preparing and just before serving.

Approximate Nutritional Values:

Serving size: 1/4 recipe
Calories: 54 calories
Fat: 0.4 grams
Carbohydrates: 12.5 grams
Protein: 0 grams
Cholesterol: 0 milligrams

BEAN AND CORN SALAD

Ingredients

4 medium sized ears of corn
1/2 head iceberg lettuce
1 medium red pepper
1/4 cup apricot preserves
3 tablespoons lime juice
1 tablespoon olive oil
1/2 teaspoon ground black pepper
1/2 teaspoon chili pepper (season to taste)
16 ounces black beans
16 ounces lima beans
1 finely chopped jalapeño (remove seeds while wearing protective gloves)

Place the ears of corn in a pan of boiling water and simmer for five minutes. Let the corn cool and then remove the kernels. Slice the lettuce and dice the red pepper and set aside. Combine the chili powder, olive oil, lime juice, and apricot preserves. Then, mix in the corn kernels, black beans, lima beans, jalapeño, lettuce, red pepper, and ground pepper. Serve chilled.

Approximate Nutritional Values:

Serving size: 1/4 recipe
Calories: 315 calories
Fat: 5 grams
Carbohydrates: 60 grams
Protein: 7 grams
Cholesterol: 0 milligrams

BERRY CHEESE BLINTZES

Ingredients

Crepes
1/2 cup egg substitute
1 cup skim milk
1 tablespoon sugar
1/2 cup wheat germ
1/2 cup all purpose flour
1 tablespoon melted margarine

Filling
1 cup nonfat ricotta cheese
1/2 cup nonfat cream cheese
1/2 cup nonfat sour cream
1/3 cup wheat germ
2 tablespoons sugar
1 teaspoon vanilla extract
nonfat nonstick cooking spray
2 cups fresh raspberries

In a food processor or blender mix the crepe ingredients for about one minute until smooth. Pour into a bowl and let stand until slightly thickened. Pour 1/4 cup of batter in a skillet which has been sprayed with nonfat cooking spray. Cook for about 45 seconds until the top of the crepe appears dry, then turn over for about 20 seconds until done.

Preheat the oven to 400° F and spray a 13 by 9-inch pan with nonfat cooking spray. In a bowl combine the ricotta and cream cheeses, then add the sour cream, wheat germ, sugar, vanilla extract and mix thoroughly. Place two tablespoons of the mixture in the middle of each crepe and fold two sides of crepe over filling. Once all the crepes are filled, place them into the pan and put into the oven for 10 to 15 minutes until heated thoroughly. Remove and top with raspberries.

Approximate Nutritional Values:

Serving size: 1/12 recipe
Calories: 136 calories
Fat: 4 grams
Carbohydrates: 15 grams
Protein: 10 grams
Cholesterol: 0 milligrams

BLACK BEANS AND RICE

Ingredients

2 cups wild rice
2 cups black beans
1 medium size tomato (chopped)
1 tablespoon chopped parsley
1/3 cup nonfat Italian salad dressing

Cook two cups of black beans and two cups of wild rice separately. Mix the cooled wild rice and black beans. Add the chopped tomato and parsley and mix thoroughly. Pour the salad dressing onto the rice, beans, and tomato combination and mix thoroughly.

Approximate Nutritional Values:

Serving size: 1/4 recipe
Calories: 215 calories
Fat: 0.6 grams
Carbohydrates: 44 grams
Protein: 8 grams
Cholesterol: 0 milligrams

BLACK-EYED PEAS*

Ingredients

1 pound unshelled black-eyed peas*
1 cup chopped onion
1 10-1/2 ounce can of chicken broth
2 cups water
2 tablespoons white wine cooking vinegar
1 tablespoon olive or canola oil
1 tablespoon lemon juice
1 teaspoon honey
1/2 teaspoon thyme
1/2 teaspoon dill
1/4 teaspoon ground pepper
2 cloves garlic (pressed)
1 cup cherry tomatoes (cut in half)
1/4 cup sliced green onions

spinach leaves (place on plate first and then add black-eyed peas)

Sauté the chopped onion for about five minutes before adding the black-eyed peas, water, and chicken broth. This should be brought to a boil and then simmered for 30 minutes until the black-eyed peas are tender. Drain and set aside.

Mix the white wine vinegar, olive oil, lemon juice, honey, dill thyme, pepper, and cloves of garlic with a wire whisk. Add this to the peas and mix in the sliced cherry tomatoes and green onions. Marinade overnight and serve on spinach leaves.

* fresh peas are always best, the peas should be tender but not soft

Approximate Nutritional Values:

Serving size: 1 cup
Calories: 120 calories
Fat: 2.5 grams
Carbohydrates: 16.8 grams
Protein: 7.5 grams
Cholesterol: 0 milligrams

BROCCOLI AND PEPPERS

Ingredients

4 cups broccoli
2 large cloves garlic
1 medium red and yellow sweet pepper

1/2 teaspoon crushed dried marjoram
1/8 teaspoon pepper

Clean and remove the seeds from red and yellow sweet peppers. Slice into small cubes to be used later. Wash the broccoli and slice the stems and cut the flowerets (trees as my children call them) into bite size pieces.

Spray a skillet with nonfat cooking spray. Heat over medium heat. Add two large cloves of minced garlic and cook for about 15 seconds. Then, add the cut sweet red and yellow peppers and broccoli. Add four to five tablespoons of water (to cover bottom of skillet) in the place of oil. Also add marjoram and pepper for seasoning. Continue to add water as needed to stir fry the vegetables. This should take approximately five minutes. Stop when vegetables are crisp and tender, but not limp.

Approximate Nutritional Values:

Serving size: 1/4 recipe
Calories: 24 calories
Fat: 0 grams
Carbohydrates: 6 grams
Protein: 3 grams
Cholesterol: 0 milligrams

BROCCOLI SALAD

Ingredients

2 pounds fresh broccoli in small pieces
12 ounces fresh mushrooms (sliced)
1 medium red onion (sliced)
2-1/4 ounce can ripe olives (drained)
1 cup nonfat italian dressing
1/3 cup shredded parmesan cheese
1/2 cup chopped celery

Mix all the ingredients together and cover. Place into the refrigerator to chill for at least two hours before serving.

Approximate Nutritional Values:

Serving size: 1/6 recipe
Calories: 148 calories
Fat: 4 grams
Carbohydrates: 18 grams
Protein: 10 grams
Cholesterol: 6 milligrams

Most of the fat can be eliminated by removing the olives from the recipe. The cholesterol is in the cheese.

BURRITO (VEGETARIAN)

Ingredients

1 medium green bell pepper
1 medium onion (chopped)
1 cup kidney beans
2 teaspoons herb seasoning
2 tablespoons tomato sauce
4 eight-inch flour tortillas
1 large tomato (chopped)
2 ounces Mozzarella cheese
1 cup nonfat plain or vanilla yogurt

Spray a skillet with nonfat cooking spray and sauté one medium green bell pepper and one medium onion until tender. In a food processor or blender puree one cup kidney beans, seasoning (herb), and tomato sauce.

Preheat your oven to about 350° F. Open four tortillas and add 1/4 of the pureed bean mix, pepper, onions, and 1/2 ounce Mozzarella cheese to each.

Roll up the tortilla and place seam side down in a baking pan which has been sprayed with nonfat nonstick cooking spray. Bake for about 10 minutes each.

Place shredded lettuce on plate and add the burrito. Top burrito with 1/4 cup nonfat plain or vanilla yogurt and/or salsa sauce (page 93) and add 1/4 sliced medium tomato beside the burrito.

Approximate Nutritional Values:

Serving size: 2 burritos
Calories: 250 calories
Fat: 4.5 grams
Carbohydrates: 32 grams
Protein: 20 grams
Cholesterol: 5 milligrams

CAPONATA (EGGPLANT SALAD)

Ingredients

1 medium eggplant (cubed)
1 small onion (chopped)
2 tablespoons white wine vinegar
1 clove garlic (pressed)
1/2 cup celery (chopped)
1/2 cup zucchini (chopped)
1 tablespoon capers
1 tablespoon tomato paste
1 tablespoon pine nuts
1/2 teaspoon dried oregano leaves
1/4 teaspoon ground pepper
1 each: medium red, yellow, and green pepper
1/3 cup olive oil

Boil water and add eggplant and cook for about 10 minutes until the eggplant is tender. Remove the eggplant from any remaining water and mix it with onion, red pepper, yellow pepper, green pepper, celery, and zucchini. In a separate bowl combine garlic, oregano, ground pepper, white wine vinegar, capers, pine nuts, and tomato paste. This mixture is then poured over the eggplant and onion mixture. Thoroughly mix everything. Cover and refrigerate overnight for best results. Stir in olive oil just before serving.

Approximate Nutritional Values:

Serving size: 1/4 recipe
Calories: 64 calories
Fat: 0.5 grams

Carbohydrates: 14 grams
Protein: 0.4 grams
Cholesterol: 0 milligrams

CARROT SALAD

Ingredients

10 shredded carrots
8 ounces of crushed pineapple (drained)
1/2 cup raisins
1/2 cup low fat vanilla or plain yogurt

This is probably the simplest recipe you'll ever find!

Mix all the ingredients together and serve.

Approximate Nutritional Values:

Serving size: 1/4 recipe
Calories: 176 calories
Fat: 0 grams
Carbohydrates: 39 grams
Protein: 5 grams
Cholesterol: 0 milligrams

CHILI (VEGETARIAN)

Ingredients

2-1/2 cups cooked soybeans
2 cups cooked kidney beans
2 cups chopped tomatoes
2 cups chopped onions
1/2 cup chopped green pepper
2 cloves minced garlic
6 ounces tomato paste
1/2 cup water
2 tablespoons chili powder (to taste)
1/2 teaspoon oregano
1/8 teaspoon ground red pepper (to taste)
4 cups brown rice

Prepare soybeans and kidney beans as shown on page 94 the day before making this recipe.

Add the soybeans, tomatoes, onions, green pepper, garlic, tomato paste, water, chili powder, oregano, and ground red pepper to a pan and bring the chili to a boil. Cover and reduce to a simmer for 2-1/2 hours until thickened. Add the kidney beans and mix thoroughly. Cook for an additional 15 to 30 minutes. Stir in brown rice which has been prepared in advance according to package instructions (limiting oils) and serve in soup bowls.

Approximate Nutritional Values:

Serving size: 1/8 recipe
Calories: 345 calories
Fat: 4.5 grams

Carbohydrates: 60 grams
Protein: 16 grams
Cholesterol: 0 milligrams

114

CHINESE NOODLES AND ASPARAGUS

Ingredients

1 teaspoon sesame seed oil
3 minced garlic cloves
2 tablespoons grated ginger
1/2 cup chicken broth
3 tablespoons Hoisin sauce
1 package Chinese noodles
1 pound fresh asparagus

In a saucepan add the sesame oil and sauté the minced garlic and ginger for about 4 to 5 minutes over medium heat. Add the chicken broth and Hoisin sauce and bring to a boil. Reduce the heat and simmer for about 3 more minutes.

Prepare the Chinese noodles according to the package instructions.

Steam the asparagus.

Place 1/4 of the Chinese noodles on a serving plate and top with 1/4 of the sauce. Add the asparagus to the side of the noodles and serve.

Approximate Nutritional Values:

Serving size: 1/4 recipe
Calories: 190 calories
Fat: 1 gram
Carbohydrates: 35 grams
Protein: 10 grams
Cholesterol: 0 milligrams

CHOCOLATE CAKE (FAT-FREE)

Ingredients

1-1/4 cups flour
1/2 cup unsweetened cocoa
1/4 cup cornstarch
1 teaspoon baking powder
1/2 teaspoon baking soda
1/2 teaspoon salt
1-1/4 cups sugar
1 cup water
1/2 cup egg substitute
1/2 cup corn syrup

Preheat your oven to 350° F and spray your 9-inch square baking pan with nonfat nonstick cooking spray.

Mix the flour, unsweetened cocoa, cornstarch, baking powder, baking soda, and salt together.

In a large bowl stir the sugar and water together until the sugar is almost dissolved, then add the egg substitute and corn syrup. Stir this until thoroughly blended. Slowly pour this into the dry ingredients prepared earlier, stirring until smooth. Pour cake mix into the baking pan and place in the oven for about 35 minutes until done. You should be able to insert a toothpick into the center of the cake and remove it without any dough/mix coming out with the toothpick. Remove from oven and allow to cool before serving.

Approximate Nutritional Values:

Serving size: 1/16 of cake
Calories: 144 calories
Fat: 0 grams
Carbohydrates: 34 grams
Protein: 2 grams
Cholesterol: 0 milligrams

Occasionally you can have your cake and eat it too !!!

CHUTNEY

Ingredients

2 small peeled and cored apples
2 small peeled and cored pears
1/2 cup raisins
1/2 cup brown sugar
3/4 teaspoon cinnamon
1/2 cup cider vinegar
1/4 cup chopped onion
1 clove minced garlic
1/2 teaspoon ginger
1/3 teaspoon allspice
1/3 teaspoon ground pepper

Mix together the apples, pears, raisins, brown sugar, cinnamon, vinegar, onion, garlic, ginger, allspice, and pepper and bring to a boil. Reduce the heat and simmer for 40 to 45 minutes until thickened. This makes an excellent sauce.

Approximate Nutritional Values:

Serving size: 2 tablespoons
Calories: 64 calories
Fat: 0 grams
Carbohydrates: 16 grams
Protein: 0 grams
Cholesterol: 0 milligrams

CORN AND BEAN SALAD

Ingredients

15 ounces black turtle beans
1 large bell pepper
1 cup whole kernel corn
4 ounces green chilies (hot or mild depending upon your taste)
2 sliced green onions

Cumin dressing: 1/2 teaspoon ground cumin, 1 clove minced garlic, 1 teaspoon grated lemon peel, and 2 tablespoons each white wine vinegar and lemon juice

Broil green bell pepper for approximately 15 to 20 minutes until charred. Seal in plastic container until cooled. Once cooled remove charred skin, remove stem and seeds, and cut remaining pepper into small cubes.

Add black turtle beans to the bell pepper once the beans have been rinsed and drained. Then, combine chilies, onions, and corn with the bell pepper and beans. Mix with the cumin dressing and refrigerate overnight. Serve chilled.

Approximate Nutritional Values:

Serving size: 1/8 recipe
Calories: 128 calories
Fat: 2 grams
Carbohydrates: 26 grams
Protein: 8 grams
Cholesterol: 0 milligrams

CORN CHOWDER

Ingredients

1/4 cup chopped onion
1/4 cup chopped red pepper
1 tablespoon flour
4 tablespoons water
2 cups skim milk
1-1/2 cups whole kernel corn
1/8 teaspoon pepper

In a non-stick skillet sauté the onion and red pepper for about four minutes until tender.

Add one tablespoon of flour to four tablespoons of water to prevent lumping of flour.

In a medium pan combine skim milk, corn, and pepper. Bring to a boil and add the onion, red pepper, and flour. Be careful to stir the flour in slowly to avoid lumps. Reduce the heat to a simmer and cook for about 5 minutes or until the corn chowder is thickened and the corn is tender. Serve warm.

Approximate Nutritional Values:

Serving size: 1/4 recipe
Calories: 146 calories
Fat: 2 grams
Carbohydrates: 26 grams
Protein: 6 grams
Cholesterol: 1 milligram

CORNMEAL MUFFINS

Ingredients

1 cup all purpose flour
1 cup cornmeal
2 tablespoons sugar
4 teaspoons baking powder
1/8 teaspoon onion salt
egg substitute the equivalent of 4 egg whites
1 cup skim milk
2 tablespoons canola oil

Preheat the oven to 425° F and spray a 12 muffin muffin pan with nonfat nonstick cooking spray.

In a mixing bowl stir in 1 cup of all purpose flour, 1 cup of corn-meal, 2 tablespoons of sugar, 4 teaspoons of baking powder, and 1/8 teaspoon of onion salt. In a separate bowl mix egg substitute, skim milk, and canola oil. Add the egg substitute mixture to the flour mix stirring the batter until smooth. Be careful not to over beat the batter. Fill each of the muffin tins until 2/3 full.

Place in the oven for about 15 minutes or until they begin to brown.

Approximate Nutritional Values:

Serving size: 1 muffin
Calories: 146 calories
Fat: 2 grams

Carbohydrates: 26 grams
Protein: 6 grams
Cholesterol: 1 milligram

CRACKED WHEAT SALAD

Ingredients

2 cups uncooked bulgur wheat (aka cracked wheat)
3 large tomatoes
1 medium onion (chopped)
1 cup parsley (chopped)
1/2 cup red bell pepper (chopped)
1/3 cup lemon juice
1-1/2 tablespoons olive oil

Add water to 2 cups of bulgur wheat until it is just covered. Let set for one hour and then drain off the excess water. Mix in the tomatoes, onion, parsley, and red bell pepper. Add the lemon juice and pepper along with the olive oil. Place in a covered bowl in the refrigerator for several hours before serving.

Approximate Nutritional Values:

Serving size: 1/12 recipe
Calories: 115 calories
Fat: 3 grams
Carbohydrates: 18 grams
Protein: 4 grams
Cholesterol: 0 milligrams

ENCHILADAS

Ingredients

8 tortillas
8 ounces pinto beans (prepared as directed on page 94)
8 ounces garbanzo beans (prepared as directed on page 94)
2 cups of shredded lettuce
1/2 cup chopped onion
1 and 1/2 cup tomato slices
1/2 cup chopped green pepper
Salsa

Preheat your oven to 350° F while mashing the pinto and gar-bonzo beans in a small bowl. You can also use a food processor to smooth the beans. Mix in the chopped onion and place two tablespoons of the mixture on a flour tortilla. Roll the tortilla and place on a nonstick (preferably glass) baking dish. Repeat this until you have rolled all eight tortillas. Pour salsa over the tortillas according to your taste. Cover the dish with aluminum foil and bake for about 20 minutes. Then, remove the foil and bake for another 5 minutes until slightly browned. Garnish each tortilla with two tomato slices and chopped green onion. Serve on a bead of shredded lettuce.

Approximate Nutritional Values:

Serving size: 1/8 recipe
Calories: 150 calories
Fat: 2.5 grams
Carbohydrates: 27 grams
Protein: 5 grams
Cholesterol: 0 milligrams

FRENCH ONION SOUP

Ingredients

2 medium sized onions sliced into rings
1 tablespoon flour
4 tablespoons water
4 cups beef broth
1/8 teaspoon ground pepper
1/4 cup croutons

Sauté two medium sized onions in a nonstick skillet until tender.

Mix one tablespoon of flour with four tablespoons of water and mix to prevent lumps.

Add 4 cups of beef broth to a pan and bring to a boil, add in the flour and water mixture, stirring constantly to prevent lumps of flour from developing. Add the onions and ground pepper. Reduce the heat to a simmer and cover, stirring occasionally for 25 to 30 minutes until the onions are soft.

Serve in soup bowl and top with croutons.

Approximate Nutritional Values:

Serving size: 1 cup
Calories: 70 calories
Fat: 1 gram
Carbohydrates: 10 grams
Protein: 5 grams
Cholesterol: 0 milligrams

FRUIT-FILLED SQUASH

Ingredients

2 medium acorn squash
2 cups chopped, unpeeled cooking apples
3/4 cup fresh cranberries
1/4 cup firmly packed brown sugar
1/4 teaspoon ground cinnamon
vegetable oil for coating only

Cut acorn squash in half and place cut side down in shallow cooking dish/pan filled with one inch of water. Place the squash in a preheated oven at 350° F for 30 minutes. Combine the apples, cranberries, brown sugar, and cinnamon in a separate bowl and set aside. After 30 minutes, remove the acorn squash from the oven and turn over. Coat the inside of the squash with vegetable oil and fill the cavities with the fruit and sugar mixture from above. Return the filled squash to the oven for 30 more minutes at 350° F, or until the squash is tender.

Approximate Nutritional Values:

Serving size: 1/4 recipe
Calories: 156 calories
Fat: 2.6 grams
Carbohydrates: 30 grams
Protein: 3 grams
Cholesterol: 0 milligrams

FRUIT KEBABS

Ingredients

1 cantaloupe
1 honeydew melon
1 watermelon
8 ounces pineapple chunks (drained)
1 pint strawberries
1 can frozen orange juice

Mix the orange juice as directed on the package. This will be used only to coat the fruits to prevent discoloration. Cube each of the above fruits, removing as many seeds as possible from the watermelon. Place two chucks of cantaloupe, honeydew melon, watermelon, pineapple, and strawberries on a skewer and lightly coat with the orange juice. Seal in an airtight bag if serving later. If serving immediately, the orange juice can be avoided.

Approximate Nutritional Values:

Serving size: 1 skewer
Calories: 30 calories
Fat: 0.1 grams
Carbohydrates: 6.7 grams
Protein: 0.5 grams
Cholesterol: 0 milligrams

FRUIT SALAD

Ingredients

1/2 honeydew melon
1 large papaya
8 ounces pineapple chunks (drained)
1 pint strawberries

Remove the seeds from one-half honeydew melon. Use a melon baller to make bite-sized pieces of melon. Mix the melon balls with one large papaya which has been cubed after its seeds have been removed. Add one pint of strawberries which have had the stems removed. Add to this 8 ounces of pineapple chunks. Mix this together with 3 tablespoons of lime juice and 1/3 cup of orange juice. Serve chilled.

Approximate Nutritional Values:

Serving size: 1/6 recipe
Calories: 128 calories
Fat: 0 grams
Carbohydrates: 31 grams
Protein: 1 gram
Cholesterol: 0 milligrams

GAZPACHO

Ingredients

1 cup chicken broth
2 large cucumbers
4 tablespoons chopped green onions
1 large sweet yellow pepper
1/2 teaspoon crushed thyme
12 rome tomatoes
1/2 cup vegetable juice cocktail
3 tablespoons red wine vinegar
1/2 teaspoon hot pepper sauce

This is a good recipe to prepare a day in advance, but is well worth the preparation. Nine tomatoes (stems removed) and one large cucumber are chopped. To this you add two tablespoons of green onions, 1/2 cup chopped sweet yellow pepper, 1/2 teaspoon crushed thyme, 1 cup chicken broth, and 1/2 cup vegetable juice. All of this is then pureed in a blender or food processor. After this it is strained until all that remains in the strainer are skins and seeds which are then discarded. Skim the foam from the juice and then add three tablespoons of red wine vinegar and 1/2 teaspoon hot pepper sauce. Of course if you like it spicy you can experiment with the hot pepper sauce.

Finally, to the above soup, add one large cucumber which has been chopped, 3 large tomatoes which have been chopped, and seeded, 1/2 cup chopped sweet yellow pepper, and two tablespoons of chopped green onions. This soup is then covered and chilled in the refrigerator overnight.

Approximate Nutritional Values:

Serving size: 1/6 recipe
Calories: 176 calories
Fat: 0 grams
Carbohydrates: 37 grams
Protein: 7 grams
Cholesterol: 0 milligrams

GOURMET RICE PILAF

Ingredients

1 small chopped onion
1 clove minced garlic
2 tablespoons water
1/4 chopped red pepper
1/4 chopped green pepper
3 green onions (chopped)
1 stalk celery (chopped)
1/2 cup frozen corn
1/2 pound sliced mushrooms
2 cups cooked brown rice (according to package instructions)

Cook the onion and garlic in a skillet sprayed with nonfat nonstick cooking spray with 1 to 2 tablespoons of water for about three minutes. Add the remaining vegetables and cook for about 3 to 5 minutes until done. Serve over the cooked brown rice.

Approximate Nutritional Values:

Serving size: 1/4 recipe
Calories: 112 calories
Fat: 0 grams
Carbohydrates: 25 grams
Protein: 3 grams
Cholesterol: 0 milligrams

GREEN PEPPERS - STUFFED

Ingredients

4 large green bell peppers
8-3/4 ounces whole kernel corn
15 ounces black beans
1 medium onion
1/3 cup long grain wild rice
1 cup water
2 tablespoons cilantro
3/4 cup reduced-fat Monterey Jack cheese

Cut the tops off four large green bell peppers. Remove the seeds from the inside and place into a pan of boiling water for four to five minutes, until the peppers are tender.

In another pan with one cup of water, add black beans, corn, chopped onion, and rice. Make certain that you have drained the vegetables if canned. Bring this mixture to a boil, then reduce the heat to a simmer and cover the pan for approximately 15 minutes or until the rice is tender. Mix this thoroughly with two tablespoons of cilantro and 3/8 cup of Monterey Jack cheese.

Take the filling and place into the four large bell peppers. The peppers should then be placed on a cooking sheet or pan which has been coated with nonfat cooking spray. The remaining Monterey Jack cheese is sprinkled on top of the peppers and they are placed into a 400° oven for approximately 5 minutes at which time the cheese will have melted on top.

Approximate Nutritional Values:
Serving size: 1/4 recipe
Calories: 270 calories
Fat: 5 grams
Carbohydrates: 45 grams
Protein: 16 grams
Cholesterol: 15 milligrams

The fat and cholesterol are primarily from the cheese. Further reductions can be made by eliminating the cheese or replacing it with parmesan cheese.

HUMMUS DIP

Ingredients

1/4 cup sesame seeds (toasted)
2 cups cooked garbanzo beans
3 tablespoons lemon juice
1/2 teaspoon cumin
4 cloves minced garlic
1/2 teaspoon water
"pinch" of cayenne
"pinch" of salt

Mix the above ingredients in a food processor or until well chopped. Use additional water, one teaspoon at a time to thin out if too thick for individual taste.

This is an excellent dip for raw vegetables such as carrots, cucumbers, green pepper, celery, and cherry tomatoes.

Approximate Nutritional Values:

Serving size: 1/8 recipe
Calories: 218 calories
Fat: 5 grams
Carbohydrates: 32 grams
Protein: 11 grams
Cholesterol: 0 milligrams

JAMBALAYA (VEGETARIAN)

Ingredients

1 small chopped green pepper
1 medium sliced stalk of celery
1 small yellow onion (chopped)
2 cloves garlic (minced)
2 cups long grain wild rice
1 cup chopped mushrooms
1 pound chopped tomatoes
1 cup chicken broth
1/4 teaspoon thyme
1/8 teaspoon allspice
1/8 teaspoon cloves
1/8 teaspoon cayenne pepper

Coat a large sauce pan with nonfat nonstick cooking spray. Over a medium heat sauté the green pepper, celery, onion, mushrooms, and garlic, adding a few drops of water as needed. Add the rice and stir occasionally. The rice should be cooked until golden in color. This should take about 7 or 8 minutes. Then, add the tomatoes with their sauce, the chicken broth, and the remaining spices and bring to a boil. Reduce the heat to a simmer and cook for about 15 minutes without a lid. Cook until the rice is tender.

Approximate Nutritional Values:
Serving size: 1/4 recipe
Calories: 338 calories
Fat: 0.3 grams
Carbohydrates: 77 grams
Protein: 6.6 grams
Cholesterol: 0 milligrams

JICAMA SALAD

Ingredients

5 ounces of lettuce (romaine, bib, etc.) or red lettuce or spinach or a combination of these

1 cup jicama strips or bean sprouts
1 cup sliced mushrooms
1/2 sweet red or yellow pepper
1/2 cup sliced water chestnuts

In a large salad mixing bowel combine jicama, water chestnuts, and peppers. This can then be mixed with the salad green of your choice. The combination should be covered and chilled before serving.

Approximate Nutritional Values:

Serving size: 1/4 recipe
Calories: 68 calories
Fat: 0 grams
Carbohydrates: 13 grams
Protein: 3 grams
Cholesterol: 0 milligrams

As always, you can add salad dressing to this but you must add the calories, fat, carbohydrates, and protein contributions to the above values. An alternative salad dressing is lemon juice.

LASAGNA (BLACK BEAN)

Ingredients

1 package whole wheat lasagna noodles
3-15 ounce cans black beans which have been drained, or
    equivalent prepared as shown on page 94
1/4 cup water
2-15 ounce containers part-skim ricotta cheese
32 ounces seasoned tomato sauce
1 teaspoon garlic salt
1 teaspoon crushed thyme
1 teaspoon ground cumin
1/2 to 1 teaspoon chili powder (according to taste)
1 cup shredded Monterey Jack cheese

Preheat the oven to 350° F and spray a 13 by 9 inch pan with nonfat cooking spray. Prepare the lasagna noodles as instructed on the package, rinse, and blot dry. In a separate bowl mix the black beans, water, garlic salt, chili powder, thyme, and cumin. Thoroughly mix until all the water is absorbed and the beans have been mashed.

Place a single layer of noodles on the bottom of the cooking pan. Cover with about 1/2 of the bean mix, then 1/2 of the ricotta cheese, and then 1/2 of the seasoned tomato sauce. Repeat this for the second layer. Cover with the remaining noodles. Sprinkle Monterey Jack cheese on top. Place the pan in the oven for 40 to 45 minutes until the edges begin to brown. Remove from the oven and let the lasagna cool for about 10 minutes before serving.

Approximate Nutritional Values:

Serving size: 1/8 recipe
Calories: 490 calories
Fat: 19 grams
Carbohydrates: 54 grams
Protein: 26 grams
Cholesterol: 25 milligrams

LASAGNA (VEGETARIAN)

Ingredients

Lasagna noodles
1 red bell pepper (sliced)
1/3 cup red cooking wine
1/2 cup chopped onion
1/4 cup basil leaves
2 cups broccoli (chopped)
1-1/3 cup mozzarella cheese
3 medium tomatoes (chopped)
15 ounces low or nonfat ricotta cheese
egg beaters—the equivalent of 1 egg white
2-3/4 cups seasoned tomato sauce
1 or 2 cloves minced garlic (according to taste)

Preheat your oven to 350° F and spray an 8-inch cooking dish with nonfat cooking spray. Prepare lasagna noodles as instructed on package, rinse, and let stand in "warm" water. Sauté the red bell pepper, onion, garlic, and cooking wine for about 6 to 7 minutes until the vegetables are tender. Then, add the tomatoes, broccoli, and basil leaves. Mix well and remove from heat. In a separate bowl mix the ricotta cheese and egg beater.

Place a layer of lasagna noodles on the bottom of the cooking dish and cover with 1/2 cup of the seasoned tomato sauce. Then cover this with two layers of lasagna noodles. On top of this place 1/2 cup of seasoned tomato sauce, then 1/3 of the ricotta cheese, 1/3 of the vegetable mix, and 1/4 cup of mozzarella cheese. Repeat this layering of noodles, sauce, ricotta cheese, vegetables, and mozzarella until all ingredients have been added. Top with the remaining seasoned tomato sauce.

Place in the oven for about 50 minutes, or until the edges bubble. Do not let noodles brown. Sprinkle remaining mozzarella cheese on top and let cook another 5 to 10 minutes or until the mozzarella cheese has melted on top. Let cool for about 10 minutes before cutting and eating.

Approximate Nutritional Values:

Serving size: 1/6 recipe
Calories: 390 calories
Fat: 12 grams
Carbohydrates: 46 grams
Protein: 24 grams
Cholesterol: 19 milligrams

LENTIL CREOLE

Ingredients

2 carrots (sliced)
1 stalk celery (sliced)
1 large onion (chopped)
1/2 pound okra (sliced)
1/4 pound fresh green beans (cut)
1/2 teaspoon sugar
1 teaspoon soy sauce
1/2 green pepper (chopped)
16 ounces tomatoes (chopped)
2 cloves garlic (minced)
1/2 teaspoon cayenne pepper
1 tablespoon red cooking wine
1 cup cooked lentils
tabasco sauce to taste

Mix all the ingredients except the lentils and tabasco sauce. Heat until boiling and then simmer for about 10 minutes. Add the lentils and simmer for about 15 more minutes. If using the tabasco sauce, season to taste.

Approximate Nutritional Values:

Serving size: 1/6 recipe
Calories: 85 calories
Fat: 1 gram
Carbohydrates: 15 grams
Protein: 4 grams
Cholesterol: 0 milligrams

LENTIL AND MUSHROOM CURRY

Ingredients

1 cup lentils
3 cups water
2 medium chopped onions
2 tablespoons chicken broth
1 teaspoon Worcestershire sauce
8 ounces sliced mushrooms
1 teaspoon curry powder
1 cup of nonfat yogurt
1 cup chopped green onions

Preheat your oven to 350° F.

Rinse lentils and place in pan with the 3 cups of water. Bring lentils to a boil, then reduce heat to a simmer and continue cooking for 40 minutes.

In a skillet sauté the onions in chicken broth. Add in the Worcestershire sauce, mushrooms, and curry powder. Continue to cook for about 5 minutes.

Mix the lentils and mushrooms together with 3/4 cup of the nonfat yogurt. Place in a baking dish in the oven for about 25 minutes and then remove. Top with the remaining yogurt and the chopped green onions.

Approximate Nutritional Values:

Serving size: 1/4 recipe
Calories: 249 calories
Fat: 0.5 grams
Carbohydrates: 44 grams
Protein: 17 grams
Cholesterol: 1 milligram

LENTIL SOUP

Ingredients

2 teaspoons instant chicken bouillon
1 cup sliced carrot
1 cup chopped celery
2 cloves minced garlic
1/2 teaspoon grated lemon peeling
1 cup dry lentils
1 medium onion
1/8 teaspoon ground red pepper (season to taste)

5 cups water

2 cups fresh chopped spinach

Rinse and set aside to drain one cup of dry lentils. Mix the drained lentils with the following ingredients: onion, celery, chicken bouillon, garlic, carrot, lemon peeling, ground red pepper. All of this should be placed into 5 cups of water in a large pan and brought to a boil. Once boiling, reduce the heat to simmering. The soup should be simmered for approximately 45 minutes with the lid on and then for 15 minutes with the lid removed. Stir in 2 cups of freshly chopped spinach.

Approximate Nutritional Values:

Serving size: 1/4 of soup
Calories: 228 calories
Fat: 0 grams
Carbohydrates: 38 grams
Protein: 18 grams
Cholesterol: 0 milligrams

MAIN DISH POTATO SOUP

Ingredients

15 ounce can dark red kidney beans (rinsed and drained)
16 new potatoes (cleaned and quartered)
3/4 cup water
2 cups vegetable mix (broccoli, green beans, pearl onions and
    red pepper)
1/3 cup plain nonfat yogurt
1 cup chopped celery
1 tablespoon fresh parsley
1 tablespoon Dijon mustard
1/8 teaspoon salt

Combine the potatoes and water in a saucepan and bring to a
boil. Cover and reduce heat and cook for 15 to 20 minutes until
the potatoes are tender, but not soft. Stir in the celery, kidney
beans, and mixed vegetables. Cook for another 4 to 5 minutes.
Drain and set aside.

Combine the remaining ingredients in a serving bowl. Add the
potato mixture and toss until coated. Serve warm.

Approximate Nutritional Values:

Serving size: 1/6 of soup
Calories: 185 calories
Fat: 1 gram
Carbohydrates: 38 grams
Protein: 6 grams
Cholesterol: 0 milligrams

MANICOTTI

Ingredients

1 cup chopped mushrooms
2 cloves minced garlic
3 large chopped shallots
10 ounces chopped spinach
3 tablespoons chicken broth
1-28 ounce can tomatoes (chopped)
1/4 cup tomato paste
1/2 teaspoon oregano
1 tablespoon basil
2 tablespoons apple juice concentrate
15 ounces nonfat ricotta cheese
1/2 cup egg beaters
3 tablespoons chopped parsley
3 tablespoons parmesan cheese
12 Manicotti tubes (prepared according to package)

Preheat your oven to 350° F. Combine the chicken broth, mushrooms, garlic, shallots, and spinach. Add the tomatoes, tomato paste, oregano, basil, and apple juice concentrate. Simmer in a pan for about 15 minutes, then set aside to cool.

Once cooled, mix the vegetables with the ricotta cheese, egg substitute, parsley, and parmesan cheese. Stuff the 12 Manicotti tubes. With the remaining sauce, layer the bottom of the baking dish, place the Manicotti tubes in the dish and cover with any remaining sauce.

Bake for about 35 minutes until sauce bubbles.

Approximate Nutritional Values:

Serving size: 1/4 recipe
Calories: 430 calories
Fat: 2 grams
Carbohydrates: 71 grams
Protein: 32 grams
Cholesterol: 4 milligrams

MEATLESS BAKED BEANS

Ingredients

1 pound dried navy beans (prepare according to page 94)
2 cups yellow onions (chopped)
1 cup green bell pepper (chopped)
4 cups water
1/2 cup molasses
1/3 cup ketchup
1/4 cup firmly packed dark brown sugar
1 tablespoon dry mustard
1/2 teaspoon chili powder
1/2 teaspoon salt
1/4 teaspoon pepper
1 teaspoon hickory smoke flavoring

Place the dried navy beans in a dutch oven and cover with water until 2 inches above the beans. Bring to a boil and then cook for another 2 minutes before removing from the heat. Cover the dutch oven and let stand for about one hour. Drain the beans.

Preheat your oven to 325° F.

Spray a saucepan with nonfat non-stick cooking spray. Add the onions and green bell pepper and sauté until tender. Remove the saucepan from the heat and add the green bell pepper and onions to the beans in the dutch oven along with 4 cups of water and the remaining ingredients. Cover and bake in the oven for about 2-1/2 hours. Uncover, mix, and bake for another 1-1/2 hours without the lid, until the beans are tender and the sauce thickens. Stir occasionally during the baking time.

Approximate Nutritional Values:

Serving size: 1/10 recipe
Calories: 253 calories
Fat: 1 gram
Carbohydrates: 55.5 grams
Protein: 5.5 grams
Cholesterol: 0 milligrams

MEXICAN RICE

Ingredients

1 cup long grain rice
1 clove minced garlic
1/2 cup onion (chopped)
1/2 cup water
1/2 cup picante sauce (season to taste)
10 ounces tomatoes (chopped)
1 cup green peas

In a nonstick skillet or one sprayed with nonfat cooking spray, sauté onions and garlic for 2 to 3 minutes over medium heat until tender but not soft. Add the cup of rice and pour in the 1/2 cup of water slowly over one minute. Stir in picante sauce and chopped tomatoes. Place a lid on the skillet and simmer on low heat for 20 to 25 minutes until the water is absorbed and the rice is tender. Remove from stove and allow to cool for about 5 minutes. Add green peas and serve.

Approximate Nutritional Values:

Serving size: 1/4 of soup
Calories: 200 calories
Fat: 3 grams
Carbohydrates: 38 grams
Protein: 5 grams
Cholesterol: 0 milligrams

MILANO RICE

Ingredients

3 cups cooked brown rice
1 tablespoon olive oil
2 tablespoons lemon juice
1 clove garlic (minced)
2 small zucchini
1 medium tomato (chopped)
1/2 teaspoon oregano
1/2 teaspoon rosemary
1/2 teaspoon ground pepper
1 to 2 tablespoons Parmesan cheese

Cook three cups of brown rice according to package instructions. Combine olive oil, lemon juice, and garlic, along with rosemary, oregano and ground pepper. Shake well—this is the salad dressing.

Slice one or two medium sized zucchini in half and remove the seeds. Cut the zucchini into strips approximately 1/4 inch wide. Place into a separate skillet coated with nonstick cooking spray and cook until tender but crisp.

Mix the zucchini, rice, and salad dressing when zucchini and rice are cooled. Sprinkle with Parmesan cheese.

Approximate Nutritional Values:

Serving size: 1/4 recipe
Calories: 315 calories
Fat: 7 grams

Carbohydrates: 45 grams
Protein: 18 grams
Cholesterol: 1 milligram

MINESTRONE SOUP

Ingredients

1 cup sliced green onions
1 freshly minced garlic clove
2 tablespoons olive oil

16 ounces tomato sauce or salsa (depending upon taste)
1 14-1/2 ounce can chicken broth
2 cups water
1 pound small red potatoes which have been quartered
1 cup sliced carrots
1 cup either yellow or orange bell pepper
1 cup sliced zucchini
18 ounces white kidney beans (see page 94)
1 teaspoon dried basil
1 teaspoon dried oregano
1 bay leaf

Cook 1 pound of small red potatoes. Quarter once cooled and set aside.

Sauté sliced green onions and minced garlic in the olive oil in a dutch oven. Then add either tomato sauce or salsa sauce, chicken broth, water, potatoes, carrots, peppers, zucchini, kidney beans, basil, oregano, and bay leaf. Bring the soup to a boil and then reduce to a simmer and cover for 30 to 40 minutes. When done, the potatoes should be tender. Remove the bay leaf and serve warm.

Approximate Nutritional Values:

Serving size: 1/6 recipe
Calories: 162 calories
Fat: 2 grams
Carbohydrates: 22 grams
Protein: 14 grams
Cholesterol: 1 milligram

MOUSSAKA (VEGETARIAN)

Ingredients

1 medium eggplant (sliced)
3/4 cup egg beaters
1 cup cooked brown rice
2 cups low fat cottage cheese
1/2 cup nonfat powdered milk
1/2 finely chopped onion
1/4 teaspoon sage
2 cups nonfat meatless spaghetti sauce
2 tablespoons parmesan cheese
1/2 cup chopped raw mushrooms

Preheat your oven to 375º F.

Cut the eggplant into 1/4 inch slices. Boil the eggplant for four to five minutes until blanched. Mix the egg substitute, rice, cottage cheese, powdered milk, onion, sage, and mushrooms.

Place one-half cup of meatless spaghetti sauce on the bottom of an 11 by 7 inch baking pan. On top of this place a layer of eggplant and then a layer of cheese mixture. Repeat these three layers until all the ingredients have been added and top with the parmesan cheese.

Bake in the oven for about 35 to 40 minutes.

Approximate Nutritional Values:

Serving size: 1/6 recipe
Calories: 234 calories
Fat: 2 grams
Carbohydrates: 36 grams
Protein: 18 grams
Cholesterol: 2 milligrams

MUSHROOM AND CELERY SOUP

Ingredients

1 tablespoon diced pimentos
4 cups sliced mushrooms
4 stalks chopped celery
4 cloves minced garlic
3 tablespoons white cooking wine
3 cups chicken broth
2 tablespoons Worcestershire sauce
1 teaspoon nutmeg
1/8 teaspoon black pepper

Add the mushrooms, celery, garlic, and white cooking wine to a saucepan. Cover and allow to cook over "low" heat for about 30 to 40 minutes until the vegetables are tender. Pour this into a food processor or blender along with half of the chicken broth and puree until smooth. Return the ingredients to the pan along with the remainder of the chicken broth. Add the Worcestershire sauce, nutmeg, and pimentos and bring to a boil and serve.

Approximate Nutritional Values:

Serving size: 1/4 recipe
Calories: 49 calories
Fat: 1 gram
Carbohydrates: 10 grams
Protein: 0 grams
Cholesterol: 0 milligrams

MUSHROOMS - STUFFED

Ingredients

1-1/2 cup bread
1/4 cup green pepper
1/4 cup onion
1/4 teaspoon pepper
1/2 teaspoon thyme leaves
1/4 teaspoon tumeric

36 medium sized mushrooms

Wash, remove stems and dry three dozen medium sized mushrooms. The stems should be finely chopped A skillet should be coated with a nonfat cooking spray to which 1/3 cup of finely chopped mushroom stems should be added, along with chopped green peppers and finely chopped onions. The mushroom stems, green peppers and onions should be stirred until tender. To this stir in finely chopped bread, thyme leaves, and tumeric, and pepper.

This stuffing should then be placed into the mushroom caps. The stuffed mushrooms should be placed in a baking pan coated with nonstick cooking spray. The filled side of the mushroom should be up so the stuffing doesn't fall out. Bake for 20 minutes at 350°.

Approximate Nutritional Values:

Serving size: 35 mushrooms
Calories: 8 calories
Fat: 0 grams

Carbohydrates: 2 grams
Protein: 0 grams
Cholesterol: 0 milligrams

NINE LAYERED SALAD

Ingredients

2/3 cup black turtle beans

1 head romaine lettuce

Salsa cruda: 1 cup chopped tomato, 1 clove garlic, 1/2 jalapño
  pepper, 2 tablespoons each mince onion, fresh
  minced cilantro, and lime juice

1 cup drained whole kernel corn

1 large peeled and sliced cucumber

2-1/4 ounce can slice black olives (drained)

3/4 cup nonfat mayonnaise and 3 tablespoons plain nonfat
  yogurt

2 ounces low fat shredded cheddar cheese

1 thinly sliced green onion

Place 2/3 cup of black turtle beans in two cups of water in a saucepan. Bring to a boil and simmer for 5 minutes. Let stand for two hours and pour off remaining water. Add two cups of fresh water and bring to a boil. Again, reduce heat but simmer for one to two hours until beans are tender. Once tender, drain and rinse.

Make salsa cruda mixture by chopping the following ingredients and mixing them together: tomato, garlic (minced), minced jalapeno pepper (seeded—wear gloves to protect hands), and minced onion, cilantro, and lime juice.

Tear romaine lettuce leaves into strips and place in bottom of bowl. Place layer of salsa cruda mix, then layer of beans and then corn.

Slice cucumber into thin slices and add as next layer followed by thin layer of olives and then a layer of romaine lettuce. Top this with three tablespoons nonfat yogurt mixed with 3/4 cup nonfat mayonnaise. Finally, top salad with 2 ounces of low fat cheddar cheese and one thinly sliced onion.

Approximate Nutritional Values:

Serving size: 1/12 recipe
Calories: 117 calories
Fat: 3 grams (olives and cheese)
Carbohydrates: 19 grams
Protein: 6 grams
Cholesterol: 3 milligrams

ORANGE AND JICAMA SALAD

Ingredients

1 cup sliced cucumber
4 seedless oranges
1 large jicama
spinach washed and torn
lemon or lime juice (according to taste)

Peel the cucumbers, oranges, and jicama and slice into 1/2 inch slices.

Place spinach leaves on plates and arrange cucumber, orange, and jicama slices. Lightly cover with either lemon juice or lime juice and serve.

Approximate Nutritional Values:

Serving size: 1/4 recipe
Calories: 60 calories
Fat: 0 grams
Carbohydrates: 15 grams
Protein: 0 grams
Cholesterol: 0 milligrams

ORANGE CHANTILLY

Ingredients

1 cup nonfat plain yogurt
1 cup fresh orange juice
1 cup nonfat nondairy whipped topping
1 small box sugar free orange gelatin

Prepare the plain yogurt by placing it into a double layer of cheese cloth and allowing it to drain for about one hour. This will drain the yogurt.

Prepare the gelatin according to instructions on the box and chill until set. Then, whip with an electric mixer until double volume—the consistency of whipped cream.

Place the orange juice in a pan and bring to a boil, reduce the heat, and simmer for about 20 minutes, swirling until a thick syrup remains—about 2 tablespoons worth.

Mix the drained yogurt and orange syrup together, then gently add the jello mixture and whipped topping with a rubber spatula.

Approximate Nutritional Values:

Serving size: 1 tablespoon
Calories: 16 calories
Fat: 0 grams
Carbohydrates: 4 grams
Protein: 0 grams
Cholesterol: 0 milligrams

ORANGE AND PAPAYA SALAD

Ingredients

1 head endive
1 lettuce your choice
1 papaya
1 grapefruit

Slice one papaya lengthwise. Section grapefruit slices and remove seeds. Slice one head of endive crosswise. Place lettuce of your choice on four chilled plates and arrange three slices of papaya and grapefruit on each plate and two slices of endive. Serve chilled.

Approximate Nutritional Values:

Serving size: 1/4 recipe
Calories: 94 calories
Fat: 2.5 grams
Carbohydrates: 16 grams
Protein: 2 grams
Cholesterol: 0 milligrams

PASTA SALAD

Ingredients

1/2 pound cooked spaghetti
1 cup broccoli florets (cooked until crisp)
2 green onions (sliced)
1 cup snow peas (cooked until tender)
1 shredded carrot
1 cucumber (sliced)

Dressing
1 teaspoon cornstarch
7 teaspoons chicken broth
1 tablespoon soy sauce
3 tablespoons white vinegar
1 tablespoon lemon juice
3 cloves minced garlic
1 teaspoon ginger root
1 teaspoon apple juice concentrate

Mix the spaghetti, broccoli, onions, snow peas, carrot, and cucumber together and then prepare the dressing. Mix the dressing ingredients in a pan and bring to a boil for one minute until thickened. Stir constantly while boiling. Let cool to room temperature. Pour the dressing over the spaghetti and vegetable salad and serve.

Approximate Nutritional Values:

Serving size: 1/4 recipe
Calories: 248 calories
Fat: 0 grams

Carbohydrates: 52 grams
Protein: 10 grams
Cholesterol: 0 milligrams

163

PEA SALAD

Ingredients

2 cups frozen or fresh peas
1/2 cup low-fat shredded cheddar cheese
1/4 cup sliced celery
2 tablespoons chopped onion
1/8 cup finely chopped sweet red pepper
1/8 cup finely chopped sweet yellow pepper
4 tablespoons nonfat plain or vanilla yogurt

Cook peas until tender. If using frozen peas use the package instructions. Cool the peas before adding to the salad.

Combine the cooled peas with the cheddar cheese, chopped celery, onion, and sweet red and yellow pepper. Chill overnight.

When ready to eat, stir in 4 tablespoons of nonfat plain or vanilla yogurt and serve.

Approximate Nutritional Values:

Serving size: 1/4 recipe
Calories: 110 calories
Fat: 2 grams
Carbohydrates: 14 grams
Protein: 9 grams
Cholesterol: 10 milligrams

PEAS AND MUSHROOMS

Ingredients

2 pounds unshelled green peas
6 ounces sliced mushrooms
1 cup pearl onions
1 teaspoon curry powder
1/2 cup chicken broth
1/2 cup nonfat plain yogurt
1 medium tomato (chopped)

Boil the unshelled peas until crisp but tender.

Sauté the mushrooms with the pearl onions and curry powder for about 10 to 15 minutes in the chicken broth, until the pearl onions are softened. Then add the peas and mix thoroughly. Continue heating until peas are also heated.

Stir in the nonfat yogurt and the chopped tomato and serve.

Approximate Nutritional Values:

Serving size: 1/4 recipe
Calories: 72 calories
Fat: 0 grams
Carbohydrates: 12 grams
Protein: 6 grams
Cholesterol: 0 milligrams

PICKLED ONIONS

Ingredients

1 large onion
1 cup white vinegar
1 cup cold water
1 tablespoon pickling spice
1 teaspoon sugar
1 clove garlic
4 whole cloves

In a large bowl mix the white vinegar, cold water, pickling spice, sugar, and garlic.

Slice the onion and separate into individual rings. Place in boiling water for about 10 seconds and remove quickly.

Place the onion rings into the vinegar mix and make certain the onions are completely covered. If not, add equal amounts of cold water and white vinegar to completely cover the onions.

Cover and place in the refrigerator and allow to stand overnight.

Approximate Nutritional Values:

Serving size: 1/4 recipe
Calories: 48 calories
Fat: 0 grams

Carbohydrates: 12 grams
Protein: 0 grams
Cholesterol: 0 milligrams

This same recipe can be used for cucumbers. Alternatively, the onions or cucumbers can be washed in cold water to clean and avoid the water boiling step.

POACHED PEARS

Ingredients

1 cup orange juice
1 teaspoon lemon juice
1 tablespoon sugar
1 cinnamon stick
2 red bartlett pears

In a nonstick skillet combine the orange juice, lemon juice, sugar, and cinnamon. Bring the mixture to a boil while removing the stems and seeds from pears. Slice each pear into eight slices and place in the skillet with the skin side up. Once the orange juice mixture is boiling, turn the heat down to a simmer and cover the skillet. Cook for about 5 minutes until the pears are tender. Remove pear slices and place in a desert cup. Continue simmering the juice until about 1/4 cup remains (about 4 to 5 minutes) and then pour the juice over the pear slices.

Approximate Nutritional Values:

Serving size: 8 pear slices
Calories: 104 calories
Fat: 0 grams
Carbohydrates: 25 grams
Protein: 1 gram
Cholesterol: 0 milligrams

POTATO AND KALE SOUP

Ingredients

5 cups water
1 large onion (chopped)
1/2 cup carrots (chopped)
3 cloves minced garlic
3 medium sized potatoes (chopped)
4 cups chopped kale (steamed)

In a large pan mix the water, onions, carrots, garlic, and potatoes. Bring the soup to a boil and cook until the potatoes are soft. Add in the steamed kale.

Remove about one-half of the soup and blenderize. Return to the remainder of the soup and simmer for about 5 more minutes before serving.

Approximate Nutritional Values:

Serving size: 6 servings
Calories: 88 calories
Fat: 0 grams
Carbohydrates: 20 grams
Protein: 2 grams
Cholesterol: 0 milligrams

POTATO PANCAKES

Ingredients

3 pounds grated potatoes
1/2 cup egg beaters
1 large onion (grated)
1/4 cup flour
1/2 tablespoon chopped chives

Grate 3 pounds of potatoes under cold water to prevent browning.

Mix the egg substitute and the grated potatoes. Add the onion, flour, and chopped chives.

Use either a nonstick skillet or a skillet sprayed with nonfat nonstick cooking spray. Add the potato pancake mix and cook until crisp.

Approximate Nutritional Values:

Serving size: 1/16 recipe
Calories: 104 calories
Fat: 0 grams
Carbohydrates: 20 grams
Protein: 6 grams
Cholesterol: 0 milligrams

POTATO SOUP

Ingredients

5 whole heads of garlic
2 cloves garlic (minced)
6 cups cubed potatoes
4 cups chicken broth
1 cup skim milk
1 cup diced onion
1 cup diced carrot
1/4 teaspoon ground pepper
1/3 cup chopped parsley
1 bay leaf

After removing the white skin from the five heads of garlic, wrap them in aluminum foil and bake for one hour at 350° F. Once they have cooled for about 10 to 15 minutes, squeeze the cloves to remove the pulp and juice. Discard the garlic skins.

Sauté the diced onion, carrot, and two cloves of minced garlic for five minutes. Add the diced potatoes, chicken broth, pepper, and bay leaf and bring the mixture to a boil. Reduce heat to a simmer for 20 minutes, until the potatoes are tender. Remove the bay leaf at this time.

Combine the potato mixture and the garlic pulp and puree. Return the puree to the pan and stir in the skim milk over low heat to prevent scalding. Once all the milk is added and the soup is warm, remove it from the stove and add freshly chopped parsley. Serve warm.

Approximate Nutritional Values:

Serving size: 1 cup
Calories: 180 calories
Fat: 1.0 grams
Carbohydrates: 36 grams
Protein: 6.5 grams
Cholesterol: 1.4 milligrams

RATATOUILLE

Ingredients

1 large onion (sliced)
3 cloves garlic (minced)
3 tablespoons chicken broth
16 ounces tomato sauce
2 teaspoons oregano
1 medium eggplant (finely chopped)
2 medium zucchini (finely chopped)
1 green pepper (chopped)
1 red pepper (chopped)
3 tablespoons hot salsa (see page 93)

In a pan soften the onions and garlic in the chicken broth. Add the tomato sauce and oregano and simmer for 15 to 20 minutes. Then, add the eggplant, zucchini, red and green pepper, and hot salsa (according to taste) and simmer for another 20 minutes.

Approximate Nutritional Values:

Serving size: 1/8 recipe
Calories: 48 calories
Fat: 0 grams
Carbohydrates: 11 grams
Protein: 1 gram
Cholesterol: 0 milligrams

This can also be used as a sauce over different pastas. Don't forget to figure out the calories, fat, carbohydrate, protein, and cholesterol of the pasta you use when planning to use the ratatouille as a sauce.

RAVIOLI (VEGETARIAN)

Ingredients

Pasta Dough

1 cup of flour
1 cup semolina flour
1/2 cup water

Filling
1 cup low fat or nonfat cottage cheese
2 cups finely chopped parsley
1/4 cup grated parmesan cheese
1/4 teaspoon nutmeg
1/2 cup skim milk
1/2 teaspoon minced garlic

Mix the filling ingredients in a large bowl and set aside.

Mix the two types of flour and make a well in the center, adding water slowly until a doughy consistency occurs and a ball of dough forms. Roll the dough out to about 1/8 inch thick sheet. Cut ravioli sized pieces of dough and drop a teaspoon full of filling into 1/2 of the pieces and cover with remaining pieces of dough. Seal the edges of the ravioli and gently drop into a pan of boiling water for about five minutes until tender. Serve.

Approximate Nutritional Values:

Serving size: 1/6 recipe
Calories: 104 calories
Fat: 0 grams

Carbohydrates: 23 grams
Protein: 3 grams
Cholesterol: 0 milligrams

RED BEANS AND RICE

Ingredients

2 15 ounce cans red beans (drained)
2 cloves minced garlic
1/2 cup chopped onion
1/2 cup sliced celery
1/2 cup chopped green pepper
1-8 ounce can tomato sauce
1/4 teaspoon ground red pepper
1/3 teaspoon tabasco sauce (according to taste)
3 cups cooked rice

This recipe works best with a dutch oven arrangement using a medium setting to heat the food. First place the garlic, onion, celery, and green pepper in the dutch oven for about two to three minutes. Then add the red beans, red pepper, tabasco sauce, and tomato sauce. The heat should be reduced to a simmer and the lid placed on the dutch oven. Cook for about 15 minutes.

Place 1/2 cup of cooked rice on each plate and then spoon on the red beans and rice.

Approximate Nutritional Values:

Serving size: 1/6 recipe
Calories: 315 calories
Fat: 3 grams
Carbohydrates: 60 grams
Protein: 12 grams
Cholesterol: 1 milligram

RED CABBAGE SLAW

Ingredients

1 medium red cabbage (shredded)
1-2/3 cups water
2 tablespoons apple juice concentrate
2 whole garlic
2 tablespoons lemon juice
1 tablespoon white wine vinegar
1/2 teaspoon ginger
3 whole cloves

Mix all the ingredients into a saucepan and simmer for about 30 to 40 minutes while occasionally stirring. Remove the garlic cloves and serve.

Approximate Nutritional Values:

Serving size: 1/4 recipe
Calories: 40 calories
Fat: 0 grams
Carbohydrates: 8 grams
Protein: 2 grams
Cholesterol: 0 milligrams

RICE PILAF

Ingredients

1 cup barley
1 cup long grain brown or wild rice
1 tablespoon cilantro
1 teaspoon lemon juice
1/3 cup pine nuts
4 cups water

Boil the water and stir in the barley and rice. Reduce the heat to low and cover the pan, allowing the barley and rice to simmer for about 45 minutes. Remove from stove and let stand for about five minutes after the water has been absorbed and the barley and rice are tender. Return the pan to low heat and stir in the lemon juice, pine nuts, and cilantro. Mix well and cook for 1 to 2 minutes until warm.

Approximate Nutritional Values:

Serving size: 1/6 recipe
Calories: 220 calories
Fat: 3 grams
Carbohydrates: 40 grams
Protein: 8 grams
Cholesterol: 0 milligrams

RIGATONI

Ingredients

1 cup cooked kidney beans (according to page 94 and package)
1 cup chopped onion
1/3 cup red cooking wine
1/2 cup chopped green pepper
2 cups pureed tomatoes
2 cloves minced garlic
1 tablespoon oregano
1/2 teaspoon thyme
1/2 cup chopped celery
1/4 teaspoon cayenne pepper (according to taste)
1 teaspoon white wine vinegar
8 ounces of rigatoni (according to package)

Prepare the kidney beans and rigatoni. In a medium saucepan add the red cooking wine and the onions and stir occasionally. Once the onions are soft, add the green pepper, tomatoes, garlic, oregano, thyme, and celery. Cover and cook for about 20 minutes without bringing to a boil. Then, add the kidney beans, cayenne pepper, and white wine vinegar and stir until warm.

Place the rigatoni on plates and add the sauce.

Approximate Nutritional Values:

Serving size: 1/12 recipe
Calories: 115 calories
Fat: 3 grams
Carbohydrates: 18 grams
Protein: 4 grams
Cholesterol: 0 milligrams

ROMAN STYLE PASTA

Ingredients

1 cup chopped parsley
2 cloves minced garlic
1 large onion (chopped)
3 green onions (chopped)
2 medium carrots (shredded)
3 tablespoons basil
1 cup chicken broth
3 large tomatoes (chopped)
3 cups of shredded cabbage
2 medium zucchini (sliced)
2 cups cooked cannellini beans
1/2 pound rigatoni (prepared according to package instructions)
1/4 cup grated parmesan
1 teaspoon oregano

In a medium saucepan blend the parsley, garlic, onions, carrots, and basil to 1/4 cup of chicken broth until soft. Then add the remainder of the chicken broth along with the tomatoes, cabbage, zucchini, and cannellini beans. Simmer for about 5 minutes until done.

Mix the rigatoni with the parmesan cheese, then add the above vegetables. Serve.

Approximate Nutritional Values:

Serving size: 1/8 recipe   Carbohydrates: 51 grams
Calories: 274 calories   Protein: 13 grams
Fat: 2 grams   Cholesterol: 2 milligrams

SAFFRON RICE

Ingredients

2 cups cooked rice
1/2 cup red pepper (chopped)
1/2 cup green pepper (chopped)
1/3 cup sliced green onions

2 tablespoons white wine vinegar
1 teaspoon olive oil
2 cloves minced garlic (adjust according to taste)

Cook two cups of rice according to package instructions, using chicken broth in the place of water and adding 1/8 teaspoon of saffron. Combine with red and green peppers and onions. Mix thoroughly.

To make the salad dressing combine vinegar, olive oil, and one or two cloves of minced garlic. This should be poured over the saffron rice and mixed.

Approximate Nutritional Values:

Serving size: 1/4 recipe
Calories: 166 calories
Fat: 2 grams
Carbohydrates: 32 grams
Protein: 5 grams
Cholesterol: 0 milligrams

SNOW PEAS AND RED PEPPER

Ingredients

1/2 cup celery (sliced)
2 cloves minced garlic
3 tablespoons chicken broth
1/2 pound sliced mushrooms
8 ounces water chestnuts
8 ounces bamboo shoots
1 pound snow peas
1 sweet red pepper (chopped)
low-salt soy sauce

In a wok, pour in the chicken broth and add garlic. Stir in the remaining vegetables and stir-fry for about four or five minutes until crisp. Add soy sauce to taste.

Approximate Nutritional Values:

Serving size: 1/6 recipe
Calories: 64 calories
Fat: 0 grams
Carbohydrates: 13 grams
Protein: 3 grams
Cholesterol: 0 milligrams

SPINACH SALAD

Ingredients

2 large navel oranges (peeled and sliced)
1/2 medium red onion
1 large bunch spinach (washed and torn)

Dressing:
1 cup skim milk with one teaspoon of vinegar added
1/4 cup orange juice
1/4 cup water
1 clove minced garlic
3 tablespoons apple cider vinegar
1/2 teaspoon sugar
"dash" of pepper

Blend the navel orange slices, red onion and, spinach. Mix the dressing ingredients and add to the salad ingredients. Mix thoroughly and serve.

Approximate Nutritional Values:

Serving size: 1/4 recipe
Calories: 84 calories
Fat: 0 grams
Carbohydrates: 17 grams
Protein: 4 grams
Cholesterol: 0 milligrams

SPINACH SOUFFLÉ

Ingredients

3 medium potatoes
1/2 cup egg substitute
2 tablespoons skim milk
2 tablespoons soy sauce
10 ounces chopped spinach
1/4 teaspoon white pepper

Preheat your oven to 375° F and spray your baking dish with nonfat nonstick cooking spray. Boil the potatoes until done.

In a food processor or blender, blend the potatoes, egg substitute, skim milk, white pepper, and soy sauce until smooth. Then, add the spinach and continue blending. Pour into a baking dish and bake for 15 to 20 minutes until puffed and slightly browned.

Approximate Nutritional Values:

Serving size: 1/4 recipe
Calories: 72 calories
Fat: 0 grams
Carbohydrates: 13 grams
Protein: 5 grams
Cholesterol: 0 milligrams

SPLIT PEA SOUP

Ingredients

1 cup chopped carrots
1/2 cup chopped onions
1 clove minced garlic

4 cups water
2 cups split peas
1 tablespoon white wine vinegar
1/2 teaspoon thyme
1/8 teaspoon black pepper (season to taste)

In a nonstick skillet sauté the carrots, onion and garlic for 3 to 4 minutes until tender. Add the carrots, onion, and garlic to a pan filled with 4 cups of water, split peas, white wine vinegar, thyme, and black pepper. Bring this to a boil and then reduce the heat and cover, allowing the soup to simmer for about one hour. Add additional water only if the soup becomes too thick. Serve warm.

Approximate Nutritional Values:

Serving size: 1/6 recipe
Calories: 192 calories
Fat: 4 grams
Carbohydrates: 28 grams
Protein: 11 grams
Cholesterol: 0 milligrams

SPRING PASTA

Ingredients

1/4 cup water
1/2 pound bow tie noodles
1/2 pound 1% cottage cheese
2 teaspoons nonfat sour cream
1 tablespoon parmesan cheese
1 teaspoon basil
1 cup peas
1 medium tomato sliced into 8 wedges
2 to 3 cups shredded lettuce

Mix the cottage cheese, sour cream, parmesan cheese, basil, and water and puree in a food processor or blender.

Prepare the bow tie noodles as instructed on the package and then mix with the peas. Place shredded lettuce on a plate and add the noodles and peas. Pour cheese sauce over and garnish with tomato wedges.

Approximate Nutritional Values:

Serving size: 1/2 recipe
Calories: 283 calories
Fat: 3 grams
Carbohydrates: 35 grams
Protein: 29 grams
Cholesterol: 3 milligrams

The fat and cholesterol in this recipe are from the 1% fat cottage cheese and the parmesan cheese.

STRAWBERRY AND MANDARIN ORANGE SALAD

Ingredients

8 to 10 cups spinach leaves
1/4 cup sliced green onions
1 11 oz can drained mandarin oranges
1 cup strawberries

Wash and rinse 8 to 10 cups of spinach leaves. Combine with green onions and place covered mixture in refrigerator for chilling. When ready to eat, arrange the spinach and onions on six plates. Place equal portions of chilled strawberries and drained mandarin oranges on each plate on top of spinach.

Approximate Nutritional Values:

Serving size: 1/6 recipe
Calories: 30 calories
Fat: 0 grams
Carbohydrates: 7 grams
Protein: 2 grams
Cholesterol: 0 milligrams

SUMMER FRUIT SOUP

Ingredients

3 cups diced honeydew melon
1/2 cup fresh orange juice
1/2 cup nonfat vanilla flavored yogurt
1 tablespoon honey
2 teaspoons fresh lime juice
2 cups diced peaches (peeled)
1 cup blueberries

Add the honeydew melon, orange juice, yogurt, honey, and lime juice to a food processor or blender and process until smooth. Pour this into a separate bowl and mix in the peaches and blueberries. Stir well, cover, and chill for several hours in the refrigerator before serving cold.

Approximate Nutritional Values:

Serving size: 1/6 recipe
Calories: 117 calories
Fat: 0.5 grams
Carbohydrates: 26 grams
Protein: 2 grams
Cholesterol: 1 milligram

SWEET POTATOES (TWICE BAKED)

Ingredients

2 large sweet potatoes
1/3 cup egg substitute
1/2 cup crushed pineapple (drained)
    save the juice
1/2 cup skim milk
1/3 cup apple (finely chopped)
"dash" paprika
"dash" parsley

Preheat your oven to 400° F and spray your baking pan with non-fat nonstick cooking spray.

Thoroughly clean sweet potatoes and cut groove along the length of each potato all the way around. Punch holes into potatoes with a fork to ensure adequate cooking. Bake in oven until tender, about 45 to 50 minutes. Remove from the oven and allow to partially cool. Cut in half lengthwise along the groove. Scoop out the sweet potato flesh and mix with the egg substitute, pineapple juice, and skim milk until you reach a stuffing consistency. To do this add the skim milk slowly—adding too much could cause the mix to liquify. Once you have obtained a stuffing consistency, stir in the pineapple and apple pieces and stuff the sweet potato shells. Sprinkle with paprika.

Bake for about 15 minutes and remove from oven. Sprinkle with parsley for garnish and serve.

Approximate Nutritional Values:

Serving size: 1/4 recipe
Calories: 100 calories
Fat: 0 grams
Carbohydrates: 22 grams
Protein: 3 grams
Cholesterol: 1 milligram

SWEET POTATO AND CARROT GNOCCHI

Ingredients

3/4 pound sweet potatoes
3 small carrots
1/4 cup nonfat plain yogurt
7 tablespoons flour
1/4 teaspoon nutmeg
1/8 teaspoon cumin
3/4 cup egg substitute
1/4 cup grated parmesan cheese
1 cup chicken broth
1/4 cup chopped parsley

Bake and peel the sweet potatoes and steam the carrots. Puree the sweet potatoes and carrots in a food processor or blender. Add in the yogurt, flour, nutmeg, cumin, egg substitute and parmesan cheese. Mix thoroughly. Take a small handful of the mixture and roll into small balls.

Drop the small balls of mix into boiling water. Once the balls, float continue to boil for another four or five minutes until tender and remove the gnocchi from the water.

Heat the chicken broth and pour over the gnocchi. Sprinkle with parsley and dash of grated parmesan cheese.

Approximate Nutritional Values:

Serving size: 1/4 recipe
Calories: 210 calories
Fat: 2 grams

Carbohydrates: 38 grams
Protein: 10 grams
Cholesterol: 1 milligram

TABBOULEH

Ingredients

1 cup bulgar wheat
2 cups water
3 tomatoes (chopped)
1 cup cucumber (chopped)
1-1/2 cup chopped parsley
1/2 cup shredded carrots

2 tablespoons olive oil
2 tablespoons lemon juice
1/4 teaspoon ground pepper

Combine the bulgar and water and allow to stand for about 30 minutes. Remove the excess water and add the tomatoes, cucumbers, parsley, and carrots. Mix thoroughly.

You can either use a low-fat or nonfat italian salad dressing or make a salad dressing by combining two tablespoons of olive oil, two tablespoons of lemon juice, and 1/4 teaspoon ground pepper. Pour the salad dressing over the tabbouleh and mix well. Chill for one to two hours before serving.

Approximate Nutritional Values:

Serving size: 1/6 recipe
Calories: 52 calories
Fat: 0 grams

Carbohydrates: 11 grams
Protein: 2 grams
Cholesterol: 0 milligrams

Some people like to add black olives to this salad. If you do you must remember that you will be adding fat.

190

TACOS (VEGETARIAN)

Ingredients

8 tortillas
16 ounces fat-free refried beans
1 cup nonfat swiss cheese (cheddar can be substituted)
2 cups shredded lettuce
1 large diced tomato
1 cup chopped green pepper
1/2 cup finely chopped purple onion
1 cup plain nonfat yogurt
Picante sauce (according to taste)

Prepare your skillet by spraying it with a nonfat nonstick cooking spray. Place each tortilla in the skillet for about 20 seconds on each side. Place all eight in a container to keep warm.

Prepare the refried beans according to instructions on the can.

Place the cheese, lettuce, diced tomato, green pepper, purple onion, picante sauce, and nonfat yogurt in separate bowls.

Place equal amounts of the cheese, lettuce, tomato, green pepper, and purple onion in each of the 8 warmed tortillas. Top with nonfat yogurt and/or picante sauce, according to individual tastes.

Approximate Nutritional Values:

Serving size: 2 tacos
Calories: 360 calories
Fat: 2 grams

Carbohydrates: 84 grams
Protein: 2 grams
Cholesterol: 6 milligrams

TACO SALAD

Ingredients

1 head shredded lettuce
2 large tomatoes (chopped)
1 small onion (finely chopped)
1/2 cup chopped green pepper
1 30 ounce can chili beans (heated according to instructions on can)

Place shredded lettuce on plate and cover with tomatoes, onions, and green pepper. Top with chili beans. Flavor with tabasco or taco sauce according to taste.

Approximate Nutritional Values:

Serving size: 1/6 recipe
Calories: 274 calories
Fat: 6 grams
Carbohydrates: 40 grams
Protein: 15 grams
Cholesterol: 0 milligrams

TOMATO SOUP

Ingredients

1 28 ounce can peeled tomatoes (low salt)
1 can evaporated skim milk (and one can of water)
4 tablespoons flour
1 cup water
1 tablespoon dried basil
1 teaspoon dried parsley
1 teaspoon onion flakes
1 teaspoon celery seed
1 teaspoon celery flakes
"dash" of pepper

Put the peeled tomatoes in a food processor or blender and process to pulp consistency, leaving small pieces of tomato. Pour this into a soup pan, add the above seasonings, and cook for about 5 to 10 minutes on medium heat. Add one can of evaporated skim milk and an equal amount of water. Heat to simmer.

Add 4 tablespoons of flour to 1 cup of water and mix thoroughly to prevent any lumps. The flour should be totally dissolved. Slowly add this to the soup while stirring. Stir until the soup thickens. Do not boil. Serve.

Approximate Nutritional Values:

Serving size: 1/6 recipe
Calories: 70 calories
Fat: 0 grams
Carbohydrates: 7 grams
Protein: 10.3 grams
Cholesterol: 0 milligrams

TORTELLINI AND VEGETABLES

Ingredients

1 red bell pepper
1 pound broccoli pieces
4 medium sized carrots
1 clove garlic
1/2 pound mushrooms
2 medium sized onions
1/2 pound pea pods
1/2 pound yellow summer squash
1/2 pound zucchini

2 tablespoons oil (safflower, sunflower, corn, soybean or canola)

2 lb. cooked tortellini

Slice onions, zucchini, squash, carrots, mushrooms, and pepper. Steam the sliced carrots for approximately four minutes. They should still be crisp when completed. Sauté one minced garlic clove in 2 tablespoons of oil. To the sautéed garlic clove add broccoli pieces, pea pods, and the sliced vegetables. Add a teaspoon of Italian seasoning to the mixture and stir frequently for 3 to 5 minutes. Again, the completed stir fry should be crisp. When completed, add cooked tortellini and serve.

Approximate Nutritional Values:

Serving size: 1/8 recipe
Calories: 377 calories
Fat: 8.5 grams

Carbohydrates: 75 grams
Protein: 0 grams
Cholesterol: 0 milligrams

VEGETABLE CURRY

Ingredients

1 pound cubed eggplant
3/4 cup chicken broth
1 teaspoon tamari
2 tablespoons curry powder
1 teaspoon cumin
3 cloves minced garlic
3 carrots (sliced)
2 cups finely chopped potatoes
1 finely chopped green pepper
1 finely chopped red pepper
1 large onion (chopped)
1 medium zucchini
2 cups chopped tomatoes (peeled)
1/4 cup tomato juice
16 ounces garbonzo beans
1/4 cup raisins
1 cup brown rice (cooked according to package instructions)

In a large pan add the cubed eggplant and 3 or 4 tablespoons of the chicken broth. Allow the eggplant to soften for about five minutes then remove to a separate bowl. Add the remaining chicken broth, tamari, curry powder, cumin and garlic. Mix the stock and ingredients for about two minutes while cooking over medium heat. Add the potatoes, red and green peppers, and onion, cooking for about five or six minutes until crisp but tender. Then, return the eggplant to the pan and add the zucchini, tomatoes with their juice, garbonzo beans, and raisins. Mix and cook for about ten minutes.

Place the previously cooked brown rice on plates and top with the vegetable curry.

Approximate Nutritional Values:

Serving size: 1/6 recipe
Calories: 210 calories
Fat: 2 grams
Carbohydrates: 40 grams
Protein: 8 grams
Cholesterol: 0 milligrams

VEGETABLE MIX

Ingredients

2 large zucchini (sliced)
4 large carrots (sliced)
1 onion (chopped)
2 cups chopped broccoli
2 cups chopped cauliflower
2 chopped tomatoes
1 green pepper (chopped)
1 red pepper (chopped)
5 cloves minced garlic
1/2 cup chicken broth
2 teaspoons basil
1 tablespoon soy sauce

Mix the vegetables together and sauté in the chicken broth until soft. Add the basil and soy sauce and cook over a medium heat for about five to ten minutes.

Approximate Nutritional Values:

Serving size: 1/4 recipe
Calories: 104 calories
Fat: 0 grams
Carbohydrates: 25 grams
Protein: 1 gram
Cholesterol: 0 milligrams

VEGETABLE SOUP

Ingredients

1 ten ounce can condensed tomato soup with one can of water
4 carrots, washed and peeled (cubed)
1 cup fresh peas
1 cup fresh corn
4 small potatoes (washed)
1 small onion (cubed)
4 stalks sliced celery

Cut carrots, potatoes, onions, and celery and put into the tomato soup once the soup is heated to a simmer. Cook until the vegetables are tender.

Approximate Nutritional Values:

Serving size: 1/4 recipe
Calories: 240 calories
Fat: 2 grams
Carbohydrates: 55 grams
Protein: 0 grams
Cholesterol: 0.2 milligrams

WALDORF SALAD

Ingredients

2 medium apples (chopped, cored)
1/2 cup sliced celery
1 cup pineapple chucks
1/2 cup raisins
1 cup skim milk yogurt

Combine the apples, celery, pineapple, and raisins. Blend in the nonfat plain or vanilla yogurt and serve on a bed of lettuce. Do not use mayonnaise or salad dressing.

Approximate Nutritional Values:

Serving size: 1/4 recipe
Calories: 115 calories
Fat: 0.5 grams
Carbohydrates: 27 grams
Protein: 0.2 grams
Cholesterol: 1 milligram

ZUCCHINI AND POTATOES

Ingredients

2 medium zucchini
3 medium potatoes
1 large chopped onion
1 large diced tomato
1/3 cup water
1 teaspoon oregano
1 teaspoon basil
1/4 teaspoon pepper

Slice cleaned, unpeeled potatoes and zucchini into 1/2 inch slices. Spray a nonstick nonfat cooking spray onto skillet. Sauté potatoes and onions for about 1 minute. Add 1/3 cup water and cover skillet, allowing the potatoes and onions 4 to 5 minutes of cooking time over "low" heat. Mix in the zucchini, oregano, basil, and pepper. Stir and cook until the vegetables are crisp but tender. Add tomato and mix for about 30 seconds. Serve warm.

Approximate Nutritional Values:

Serving size: 1/6 recipe
Calories: 146 calories
Fat: 0.3 grams
Carbohydrates: 33.5 grams
Protein: 2.4 grams
Cholesterol: 0 milligrams

ZUCCHINI BOATS

Ingredients

2 medium zucchini
1 teaspoon canola oil
1/2 cup chopped onion
1 cup fresh chopped mushrooms
1 clove minced garlic
1 medium chopped tomato
1/8 teaspoon pepper (season to taste)
2 tablespoons grated parmesan cheese
2 tablespoons croutons

Preheat your oven to 325° F. Slice zucchini in half lengthwise and remove the seeds. Spray skillet with nonfat cooking spray (or use a nonstick skillet) and add the garlic and chopped onion. Stir for about 2 to 3 minutes until onion is crisp but tender. Mix in mushrooms and continue for another 2 to 3 minutes. Remove skillet from stove and stir in the tomato and pepper. Mix in croutons. Divide the mixture into the four zucchini boats and place into a baking pan and cover with aluminum foil. Place the pan in the oven and bake for about 30 minutes until zucchini is crisp but tender. Sprinkle with parmesan cheese and allow to cool for 5 minutes before serving.

Approximate Nutritional Values:

Serving size: one zucchini boat
Calories: 40 calories
Fat: 1 grams

Carbohydrates: 6 grams
Protein: 2 grams
Cholesterol: 0 milligrams

ZUCCHINI BREAD

Dry ingredients
2 cups white unbleached flour
1 cup whole wheat pastry flour
1 teaspoon baking soda
1 teaspoon baking powder
1/4 teaspoon salt
1 cup sugar
1 teaspoon cinnamon
"dash" nutmeg

Other ingredients
1 tablespoon egg beaters (or equivalent) combined with 4
    tablespoons water
1 teaspoon vanilla extract
1 cup skim milk
1/2 cup applesauce (performs function of oil)
4 small zucchini (grated)

Preheat your oven to 325° F. Mix the white unbleached flour, wheat pastry flour, baking soda, baking powder, salt, sugar, cinnamon, and nutmeg together in a large mixing bowl. In the center of the mixture make a well for the wet ingredients. In another bowl mix the wet ingredients consisting of egg beaters (or equivalent), vanilla extract, skim milk, applesauce, and zucchini. Add the wet ingredients to the well made in the dry ingredients and mix until thoroughly blended. Pour the batter into a 5 by 9 inch baking pan which has been sprayed with nonstick cooking spray. Bake the bread for about 60 minutes until done in the center. Remove and allow to cool before slicing.

Approximate Nutritional Values:

Serving size: 1/2 inch slice
Calories: 138 calories
Fat: 0.7 grams
Carbohydrates: 29 grams
Protein: 4 grams
Cholesterol: 11 milligrams

ZUCCHINI, EGGPLANT, AND TOMATOES

Dry ingredients

1 medium sliced eggplant
1 medium sliced zucchini
2 medium sliced tomatoes
1 medium sliced onion
1/4 teaspoon thyme
1/4 teaspoon oregano
1/4 cup chicken broth
3 cloves minced garlic

Preheat your oven to 400° F and spray a baking dish with nonfat non-stick cooking spray. Place a layer of eggplant, then zucchini, then tomatoes, then onions, and repeat until all the vegetables have been added to the baking dish. Combine the thyme, oregano, broth, and garlic and pour over the vegetables. Cover the dish and cook for about 30 minutes.

Approximate Nutritional Values:

Serving size: 1/6 recipe
Calories: 86 calories
Fat: 0 grams
Carbohydrates: 17 grams
Protein: 4.5 grams
Cholesterol: 0 milligrams

The recipes in this chapter represent some basic recipes which you can use to build a healthier diet. Each person has individual likes and dislikes—just ask any parent with two or more children. Fortunately, these recipes, as well as any others you find, can be adjusted to your own taste. Once a recipe is changed you need to remember that the calories, fat, carbohydrates, protein and cholesterol in the recipe will also change. You should always look at what you're adding or removing from a recipe and determine what the effect will be on the nutritional value. Sometimes you can add a lot of something (fresh fruit and vegetables) without having to add a lot of calories, fat, and cholesterol, while other times adding just a little (olives and meats) can significantly increase your calories, fats, and cholesterol.

Taking individual recipes and bringing them together to make a meal requires a certain amount of talent and experience. This is part of the reason why some restaurants are successful while others are not. Sometimes you need a finishing touch or something with some color to round out the menu. For that reason I would like to end this chapter with some suggestions for grilling fruits and vegetables which are not only good for you but add color and aroma which can turn an average meal into something special.

Grilling can be done over an open barbecue pit, propane grill, or grill in your kitchen and has become quite popular again in recent years. You need to spray the grill surface with a nonfat nonstick cooking spray before grilling. Foods can either be placed on the grill or on skewers, with space between the pieces of fruit and vegetables to allow the heat to grill all sides thoroughly. The following times are "suggestions" for the amount of time you will probably need to grill the following foods. The foods should be firm and not limp when you are done grilling. You should turn the food over half way through grilling.

GRILLING 1/2-INCH SLICES

Food	Total Grilling Time (Minutes)
Apples	10
Chayote Squash	10
Corn (Ears)	18
Eggplant	25
Green Bell Pepper	10
Green Onions (whole)	10
Honeydew Melon	10
Jicama	20
Muskmelons	10
Onions	15
Orange Bell Pepper	10
Papaya	15
Pears	10
Pineapple	15
Potatoes	15
Red Bell Pepper	10
Star-Fruit	10
Tomatoes	10
Yellow Bell Pepper	10
Yellow Squash	10
Zucchini Squash	10

Many people are used to adding something to the foods which they barbecue, although as a patient of mine who owns a barbecue restaurant once told me, barbecuing is the way you prepare the food, not the sauce or topping you put on it. I think you will find that either lime or lemon juice provides an excellent baste for fruits and vegetables and you don't need oil. Coarsely ground black pepper is another good seasoning for vegetables and can be added once on the grill.

Exercise, Alcohol, and Your Cholesterol

I f you survived a heart attack in the 1950s and 60s, you could expect to spend a week or better in an intensive care unit where you would not be allowed to exert yourself because of a fear that you would have another heart attack. Today, we now appreciate the fact that the heart is a muscle, which benefits from a certain amount of exercise. While the level of activity is minimal during the first few days following a heart attack, we now use a step by step approach to increasing your physical activity prior to leaving the hospital, typically seven to ten days after you are admitted to the hospital.

There is more than one type of exercise, which physiologists and the medical profession refer to as isotonic and isometric. It is the isometric form of exercise, like weight lifting, that is without appreciable benefit for the heart and may actually cause problems. Isotonic exercise does have beneficial effects and includes activities like walking, running, swimming, bicycling, et cetera. Like all things however, there are some well known cases of individuals over exercising and having health problems as a result.

YOUR HEART IS A MUSCLE

More important than the type of isotonic exercise you do is the fact that you are doing something. After all, you are trying to tone your heart muscle and not prepare for the Olympic games. Additionally, exercise is an excellent way to lose calories, although it is much more difficult to use up calories (chapter 2) than to not eat them. One of the best exercises you can probably do is to push yourself away from the table and exercise your will power.

PUSHING AWAY FROM THE TABLE
IS A GOOD EXERCISE

Appendix A lists the number of calories you would use for a variety of activities based upon your body weight. For example, if you weigh 220 pounds and you walk at 5.3 mph for one hour, you will use up 928 calories.

$$928 \text{ calories} =$$

$$(220 \text{ pounds}) \, (4.22 \text{ calories/hour/pound}) \, (\text{one hour})$$

If you only exercise for 20 minutes, you're only going to use up 1/3 as many calories, since you don't get credit for a full hour of exercise if you don't exercise for a full hour.

While you can get almost as many opinions on how much exercise you should do as the number of people you ask, I suggest the following seven points to my patients.

1) Try to exercise three to four times a week.

2) Begin your exercise session by stretching for 15 to 20 minutes.

3) Do some type of aerobic, isotonic exercise for 30 minutes. This can be walking, jogging, running, swimming, bicycling, et cetera.

4) After exercising you should have a cool down period where you stretch for 15 to 20 minutes.

5) As your exercise tolerance increases, you can increase the number of times you exercise to five, six, or perhaps seven days a week.

6) Also as you become stronger, you may want to increase your exercise period to one hour. You will still need your warm-up (2) and cool down (4) periods.

7) Listen to your body. If you get chest pain, short of breath, or have other problems—STOP and let your doctor know.

Prior to beginning any exercise program you should check with your doctor and get his/her recommendations for you. Once you have begun an exercise program, follow your doctor's instructions.

Many people are not able to run, swim, or bicycle for one reason or another. Walking, however, is still an excellent physical exercise. Walking can also be done in the shallow end of a swimming pool. The water can help support your weight which can be particularly important if you have arthritis or are overweight. As many people now know, doing some kind of exercise like walking is much better than doing nothing. Many cities now have malls or recreation centers where people can walk inside during bad weather. It's more important to do some type of activity on a regular basis, than nothing at all.

**IT IS BETTER TO DO A LITTLE EXERCISE
THAN NO EXERCISE**

Some people are concerned about the number of calories they use up and believe that if they can't run, they can't possibly use up enough calories to make it worth the exercise. It is true that people who run for an hour will use up more calories than people who walk. In fact, the faster you run, the more calories you'll use up while you're running. This is partly because while you're running you will be going farther. Most people exercise for a certain amount of time or for a certain distance. If the runner runs until he/she has run five miles, they will use up about the same amount of calories as the person who walks five miles. It simply takes the walker longer to cover the five mile distance.

We know that exercise can increase your HDL-3 cholesterol (chapter one) if you exercise for approximately one hour each day. However, the increases tend to be minimal with changes of perhaps five mg/dl. So if your blood HDL cholesterol begins at 35, you might see it increase to 40 mg/dl after several months of daily exercise. While you may feel better about your number, you are probably having more effect by toning your muscles (including your heart) and using up calories which can help reduce your LDL-cholesterol by using up stored (fat) calories.

**EXERCISE INCREASES YOUR HDL CHOLESTEROL
BUT MORE IMPORTANTLY TONES YOUR BODY
AND USES UP CALORIES**

Mild to moderate consumption of alcohol has been shown to slightly increase HDL-2 levels, although the results are no more impressive than changes seen with exercise. Drinking more alcohol does not cause further increases in HDL-2 cholesterol. Alcohol also has about seven calories a gram (chapter three) and provides a lot of excess calories which can increase (chapter six) your cholesterol level. The problems associated with drinking too much alcohol can fill a book. The most important thing to remember about alcohol is:

> **ALCOHOL IS NOT A DRUG TREATMENT**
> **FOR HIGH CHOLESTEROL**

Medications

There is a considerable amount of misinformation about what medications can and can not do. Medicines are used to help us either by working with or against how our bodies are supposed to work. There are no "magic bullets." When physicians use medicines to treat high cholesterol or triglyceride levels, we are using drugs designed to 1) reduce the speed at which cholesterol is made, 2) increase the breakdown of triglycerides, 3) remove cholesterol in our intestines, or 4) enhance the removal of cholesterol. Each medication tends to work by one of the four approaches. Some of these drugs are better understood than others.

As we saw in chapter eight, the use of these medicines without changing your diet, will result in decreases in cholesterol of approximately 12 to 18%. This means that if your cholesterol is the same as the national average for Americans, then even if you obtain an 18% eduction in your cholesterol, you will still be higher than the recommended 200 mg/dl guidelines.

> IF YOU TRY TO REDUCE YOUR CHOLESTEROL
> WITH MEDICATIONS ALONE AND REFUSE TO
> IMPROVE YOUR DIET, YOU PROBABLY WILL
> NOT BE HAPPY WITH THE RESULTS

By changing their diets to fruits and vegetables with limited grains or vitamin (B-12) supplements, our patients reduced their cholesterol and triglyceride levels by 50 to 100 mg/dl over the course of six months and frequently sooner. Improving the diet and taking appropriate medications when indicated, yielded the fastest results. Many people, however, are able to make the necessary changes in their diet and will probably never need medications to reduce their cholesterol and reduce their risk of heart disease.

> MOST PEOPLE CAN REDUCE THEIR CHOLESTEROL
> WITHOUT DRUGS AND REDUCE THEIR
> RISK OF HEART DISEASE

Determining the presence or absence of coronary artery disease, particularly for those people who have no symptoms (chest pain, shortness of breath, etc.) is in my opinion best accomplished with Positron Emission Tomography (PET). This test is not only extremely accurate, but non-invasive, relatively inexpensive, and does not require admission to a hospital.

> DETECTION OF CORONARY ARTERY DISEASE IN
> PEOPLE WITHOUT SYMPTOMS IS IN MY OPINION
> BEST ACCOMPLISHED WITH POSITRON
> EMISSION TOMOGRAPHY (PET) IMAGING

In this chapter we will look at the five major groups of medicines used to reduce cholesterol and triglyceride levels. Medicines which reduce one type of your cholesterol may be useless for other types. These five groups are:

Hypolipidemic Medications
Currently Available

1) Bile Acid Sequestrants

COLESTID
QUESTRAN

2) Fibric Acid Derivatives

ATROMID-S
LOPID

3) HMG Co-A (3-hydroxy-3-methylglutaryl-coenzyme A) Reductase Inhibitor

LESCOL
MEVACOR
PRAVACHOL
ZOCOR
ATORVASTATIN

4) Nicotinic Acid

NICOBID
NICOLAR

5) Other

LORELCO

Of the twelve medications shown above each is used for specific types of cholesterol and can have certain problems called "side effects." Side effects are problems caused by a drug which is different from the intended purpose of the drug and may or may not be a significant problem.

Bile Acid Sequestrants

These medicines has been available for the last 10 to 20 years, and despite there being two different brands, they essentially work in a similar way.

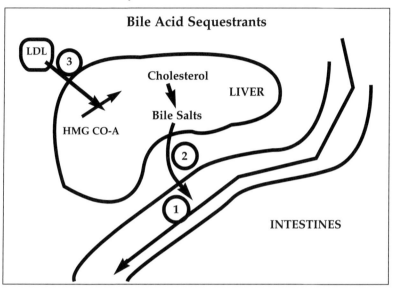

These medicines are taken two or three times a day before meals to help absorb bile salts from the intestines. The medicine must be mixed with water or juice to allow it to be safely drank. Once in the intestines (step 1) it will "bind" (attach itself) to the bile salts (step 2), removing cholesterol from the liver, causing the liver to remove more LDL from the blood (step 3) where the liver then makes more cholesterol. It is also true that these drugs may bind to other medicines you are taking if taken at the same time, reducing the amount absorbed by your body. For that reason your doctor or pharmacist should instruct you when to take your other medications. A good example of this drug interaction is digoxin, which is given to heart patients for a variety of reasons. If digoxin and bile acid sequestrants are taken together, the digoxin will not be as well absorbed by your body which may produce other problems.

| ALWAYS CHECK WITH YOUR DOCTOR OR |
| PHARMACIST ABOUT DRUG INTERACTIONS |

The maximum benefit of these drugs will usually occur in the first few weeks with LDL cholesterol levels tending to decrease. However, the liver is designed with several functions, including making cholesterol (chapter one). Since the liver can take in more LDL cholesterol, it will be able to increase the amount of VLDL cholesterol it makes and releases back into the blood by as much as 20%. Therefore, you could actually see an increase in your cholesterol level.

| ALWAYS TELL YOUR DOCTOR IF YOU ARE HAVING |
| PROBLEMS AFTER TAKING A MEDICATION |

The most frequently seen problems with these medicines include constipation, exacerbation of hemorrhoids, stomach and intestinal problems, gallstones, muscle aches and pains, headaches, dizziness, fatigue, weakness, and other problems which you should discuss with your doctor and/or pharmacist. Many of these problems can be dealt with effectively if identified. One additional note of caution includes people who have an inherited (genetic) problem known as phenylketonuria (PKU). Colestid contains phenylalanine and should not be used by people with PKU.

Fibric Acid Derivatives

The fibric acid derivatives, of which there are currently two in the United States, work by increasing the activity of lipoprotein lipase (chapter one) which increases the speed at which VLDL is converted to IDL and then LDL.

These medications are primarily used to treat elevated triglyceride levels since they work by decreasing VLDL. While some people believe these drugs may decrease LDL cholesterol, there are many studies which do not support this. The major benefit appears to be reducing triglyceride levels with mixed results for LDL.

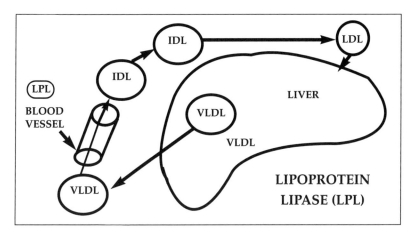

The fibric acid derivatives, like the bile acid sequestrants are usually taken twice a day before meals. The most common side effects are related to liver and gallbladder problems as well as muscle aches and pains. Blood must be checked to determine whether there are any problems with the liver or muscles while taking these medicines. The risk of problems with muscle irritation increases when fibric acid drugs are used with other medicines, particularly the HMG Co-A reductase inhibitors.

**FIBRIC ACID DRUGS AND HMG Co-A INHIBITORS
MUST BE WATCHED CLOSELY, ESPECIALLY
WHEN TAKEN TOGETHER**

Blurred vision, increases in blood sugar—a potential problem for diabetics—and gallstones can occur. You also have to be careful about taking other medications while using these medicines and should talk with your doctor or pharmacist about possible drug interactions. One example of a problem which can occur exists for people taking the drug coumadin (warfarin) which is used to reduce the clotting tendency of your blood. The combination of these medicines can result in an increased tendency to bleed. Careful monitoring by your doctor is important if you are taking both coumadin and lopid or atromid-S.

One final note of caution, the World Health Organization (WHO) conducted a study and discovered that there was a 44% increase in deaths for people who were taking atromid-S (clofibrate) when compared to people who took no medication. Many of these deaths were associated with cancers, pancreatitis, and other health problems. The use of clofibrate tends to be limited to a small group of people with specific problems.

CLOFIBRATE HAS BEEN ASSOCIATED WITH AN INCREASE IN CERTAIN TYPES OF CANCER

HMG Co-A (3-hydroxy-3-methylglutaryl-coenzyme A) Reductase Inhibitors

This group of drugs is the newest and probably the most promising for treating high cholesterol. At least one of these medications has been shown to significantly reduce the chance of a second heart attack. The goal of course is to reduce the possibility of the first or any heart attack.

The best way to understand these drugs is to consider a chain. The weakest link in a chain determines its strength because once the weakest link breaks the chain can no longer do its job. Another comparison is to look at an assembly line. As long as all the people are hard working, production continues uninterrupted. But what if one of the workers becomes sick, lazy, or can not work as hard as everyone else? The rate of production slows down to the speed of the slowest worker who then determines the overall speed of the operation. If the workers at the beginning of the production line make extra product, then a surplus exists which can only be passed down the production line at the speed of the slowest worker. Similarly, people who are waiting for the slowest worker to send them products for completion will have to wait even if they have nothing else to do. In chemistry or biology, this weakest link in a chain or slowest worker is called the "rate determining step," because the rate/speed at which something is made is determined by this weakest or slowest part or chemical reaction. If this slowest part can be slowed down further, then cholesterol will not be made as fast as it might normally be made by the liver. In the liver, this rate limiting step is the enzyme:

3-hydroxy-3-methylglutaryl-coenzyme A

The name of this enzyme is so long and difficult to remember that many people call it HMG Co-A reductase and the drugs which slow it down are called HMG Co-A reductase inhibitors. When these drugs slow down the ability of the liver to make cholesterol then cholesterol levels should decrease. However, these drugs can not prevent the liver from making cholesterol, only slow it down. These medicines have their largest effect if they are slowing the liver down when it is trying to make cholesterol.

As I mentioned in chapter two, I advise my patients not to eat after 7:00 P.M. so they will have sufficient time to use up a majority of the calories from their evening meal before going to bed. Eating later tends to leave calories for the liver to turn into fat and cholesterol while you are sleeping. The majority of cholesterol appears to be made while people are sleeping and it is at these hours that you would want these medicines to be slowing down the liver's ability to make cholesterol. There are some differences in the time of day you need to take these different medicines to have their maximum effect. You should check with your doctor or pharmacist concerning when they would like you to take your different medications.

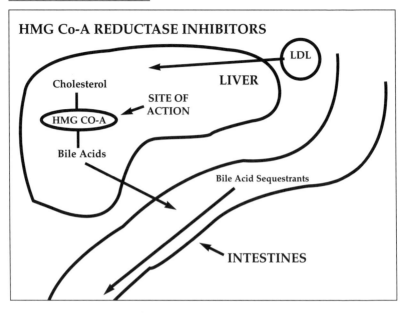

HMG Co-A REDUCTASE INHIBITORS

LDL

Cholesterol   LIVER

SITE OF
ACTION

HMG CO-A

Bile Acids

Bile Acid Sequestrants

INTESTINES

**YOU SHOULD AVOID EATING LATE
IN THE EVENING**

Usually, these drugs are taken once or twice a day. Blood work must be checked periodically to determine if you are having problems taking these medicines. Other medicines which depend upon the liver may react with the HMG Co-A reductase inhibitors. These include erythromycin antibiotics, cyclosporine used in transplant recipients, niacin, and the fibric acid drugs. The combined use of the fibric acid drugs in addition to HMG Co-A reductase inhibitors are quite effective when used in addition to changes in your diet. Some of the HMG Co-A reductase inhibitors have fewer side effects when used with the fibric acid drugs and one of these drugs in particular may improve blood flow for reasons which go beyond the scope of this book. You should check with your doctor concerning which of these medicines if any he/she would suggest.

HMG Co-A REDUCTASE INHIBITORS AND BILE ACID SEQUESTRANTS

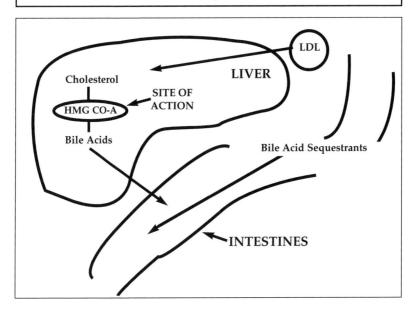

Unlike the previously mentioned medicines, these drugs have been shown to improve LDL, HDL, and triglyceride levels. The effect of these drugs, like any other drug used to treat high cholesterol, is not as promising if you do not make the necessary changes in your diet to reduce your cholesterol, fat, and calorie intake. After all, not even the strongest chain in the world or the fastest worker can stand the strain if more and more work (cholesterol, fat, calories) is presented. Remember, these medications help but they do not cure your eating habits.

IF YOU ARE SERIOUS ABOUT CHANGING YOUR CHOLESTEROL YOU NEED TO CHANGE YOUR DIET

Nicotinic Acid

There are two medications which contain niacin, not nicotine. Their primary effect appears to be one of increasing HDL cholesterol by as much as twenty-five percent, although reports vary. The effect upon the remaining types of the cholesterol appears less impressive.

People who are going to use nicotinic acid need to be aware that there are several potential problems associated with its use. A common problem is flushing, which can frequently be prevented or limited by taking an aspirin one-half hour before the niacin. Niacin should be taken with meals to reduce stomach irritation. There can also be problems with increases in glucose (blood sugar) which may present a problem for diabetics. People with gout may have more frequent episodes if they take nicotinic acid. Problems with heart rhythms have also been seen and could result in life threatening problems. It should not be given to people who have asthma, rhythm problems of the heart, inflammatory bowel disease, or liver disease. Like all drugs, careful monitoring of these medicines is necessary.

**NICOTINC ACID CAN CAUSE PROBLEMS
WITH HEART RHYTHM**

Other

This group currently includes only Lorelco. Lorelco (probucol) has been shown to decrease LDL cholesterol and probably has some antioxidant (chapter seven) effect upon LDL cholesterol. It is frequently taken twice a day. Because of the problems with serious heart rhythms, electrocardiograms (ECG/EKG) should be obtained before beginning this medication. Problems with lightheadedness and passing out could indicate problems with this drug. Because of problems with certain antidepressant drugs, people taking tricyclic antidepressants probably should not take lorelco. Finally, HDL cholesterol has been shown to decrease while taking this drug.

LORELCO MAY INTERACT WITH TRICYCLIC
ANTIDEPRESSANT MEDICATIONS TO PRODUCE
ADVERSE EFFECTS

Other medications may either increase or decrease your cholesterol. Some of the angiotensin converting enzyme inhibitor (ACE) drugs used for heart failure and high blood pressure tend to decrease cholesterol by a method which currently is not understood. All medications have potential problems which must be balanced against the expected benefit. For the medicines mentioned in this chapter, the desired result is to lower cholesterol and triglyceride levels and reduce the risk of coronary artery disease. However, because of the potential problems, costs, and limited effect (chapter eight) when these medicines as used for people who do not or will not make changes in their diet, we have to seriously ask ourselves what the role of these drugs are in this group of people and whether the benefits outweigh the potential risks. This is a question which you must ask your doctor or answer yourself.

Conclusion

Throughout this book we have looked at the make-up of cholesterol as well as where it comes from and goes in our bodies. We have seen why we make it and the harm that excess cholesterol can do to our body and the arteries of our heart. Using your weight and activity level, you can now estimate how many calories you need (appendix C and F) to either maintain or lose weight. Learning to read food labels properly (appendix D) will allow you to determine how many calories you are getting from proteins, carbohydrates, and fats, so that you can make better decisions about the types of foods you are going to eat.

> **THERE ARE NO STUDIES SHOWING THAT YOU CAN HAVE TOO LOW A CHOLESTEROL LEVEL**

Where once there was felt to be little hope in controlling cholesterol, we now know that the majority of people *can* successfully reduce their cholesterol levels and risk of heart disease by making changes in their diet and other risk factors. If you're looking for medications to do the work for you, you'll probably be disappointed because the effect of these medications is blunted if you are not willing to make the changes in your diet. Since you are what you eat, if you eat foods high in fat and cholesterol, or you eat more calories than you need, your body—including the arteries of your heart, brain, et cetera—will eventually show it.

> THERE HAS NEVER BEEN A STUDY SUGGESTING THAT
> HIGH CHOLESTEROL LEVELS ARE GOOD FOR YOU

Changing your diet is something only you can do, but it effects your family as well as yourself. Despite all the advances in medicine, there is nothing a physician or health care provider can do that will have the same beneficial impact on your health. Remember, there has never been a study showing benefits from high cholesterol and triglyceride levels. No one has ever said that being overweight would make you healthier or live longer. In fact, the evidence suggests the opposite. At the request of many of my patients I have developed this book to answer some basic questions about cholesterol and weight as well as provide some ideas for better meals using healthy foods. It is my hope that this book has provided such insight and information.

How to Bypass Your Bypass

Appendix A. Calories consumed by a variety of activities

Activity	Calories per pound per hour *
sleeping	0.43
awake, lying down	0.50
sitting still, reading	0.65
listening to the radio	0.65
watching television	0.65
reading aloud	0.69
standing relaxed	0.69
doing homework	0.70
sewing by hand	0.72
standing at attention	0.74
knitting, writing	0.75
playing cards	0.75
singing	0.79
eating	0.80
typing very fast	0.91
ironing	0.93
washing dishes	0.93
making beds	1.00
sweeping	1.09
"light" exercise	1.10
walking at 2.6 mph	1.30
"active" exercise	1.90
walking at 3.7 mph	1.95
bowling	2.25
golfing	2.50
"severe" exercise	2.90
sawing wood	3.12
swimming	3.25

* multiply by your weight in pounds for each hour of activity

Activity	Calories per pound per hour *
playing tennis	3.50
running at 5.3 mph	3.70
bicycling, dancing	3.75
skiing	3.75
"very severe" exercise	3.90
football	4.00
walking at 5.3 mph	4.22

* multiply by your weight in pounds for each hour of activity

Appendix B. Desired Weights by Height. (Normogram)

To determine whether you are at the correct weight for your height, draw a line from the weight ruler on the left to your height on the right ruler. Pay attention to kilograms versus pounds and centimeters versus inches. Then read were the line crosses using the middle ruler. Note that to the left of the middle ruler is the 18 to 35 age group, while the greater than 35 year old age group is to the right of the middle scale. To determine your ideal body weight, draw a line from the height ruler on the far right through the "good weight" region for the middle ruler and continue this line to the weight ruler on the far left. Then read the weight from the weight ruler and you know what you need to weigh for your height to have a "good weight."

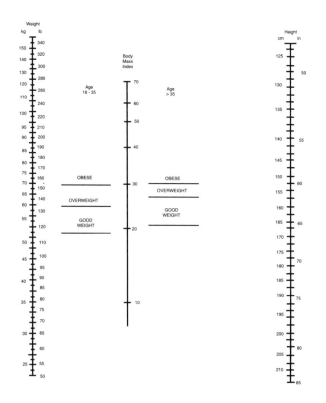

Appendix C. How many calories* can you eat each day if you are trying to lose one pound in a week.

Current Weight in Pounds	Sedentary Lifestyle	Moderately Active Lifestyle	Very Active Lifestyle
120	1,063	1,183	1,303
130	1,193	1,323	1,453
140	1,323	1,463	1,603
150	1,453	1,603	1,753
160	1,583	1,743	1,903
170	1,713	1,883	2,053
180	1,843	2,023	2,203
190	1,973	2,163	2,353
200	2,103	2,303	2,503
210	2,233	2,443	2,653
220	2,363	2,583	2,803
230	2,493	2,723	2,953
240	2,623	2,863	3,103
250	2,753	3,003	3,252
260	2,883	3,143	3,403
270	3,013	3,283	3,553
280	3,143	3,423	3,703
290	3,273	3,563	3,853
300	3,403	3,703	4,003
310	3,533	3843	4,153
320	3,663	3,983	4,303
330	3,793	4,123	4,453
340	3,923	4,263	4,603
350	4,053	4,403	4,753
360	4,183	4,543	4,903

*As described in chapter two, some people may require fewer calories each day to reduce their weight.

How to Bypass Your Bypass

Current Weight in Pounds	Sedentary Lifestyle	Moderately Active Lifestyle	Very Active Lifestyle
370	4,313	4,683	5,053
380	4,443	4,823	5,203
390	4,573	4,963	5,353
400	4,703	5,103	5,503

Appendix D. Reading Food Labels

The following example explains how to determine how many calories come from fat, protein, and carbohydrates.

Serving size: 8 oz of 2 % milk
Calories per serving:120,   Fat calories 45

Total Fat: 5 gram,   8 %
    Saturated Fat: 3.5 grams,   18 %
Cholesterol: 25 milligrams
Sodium: 110 milligrams
Total carbohydrates: 11 grams
    Fiber: 0 grams
    Sugars: 11 grams
    Protein: 8 grams

	Total Grams	X	Calories per Gram	=	Total Calories
TOTAL CALORIES PER SERVING (Estimate)					120
TOTAL GRAMS OF PROTEIN	8	X	4	=	32
TOTAL GRAMS OF CARBOHYDRATES	11	X	4	=	44
TOTAL GRAMS OF FAT	5	X	9	=	45
Total Calculated Calories					121

How to Bypass Your Bypass

To determine the percentage of calories from fat:

$$\frac{\text{total fat calories}}{\text{total calories}}$$

In this case the **percentage of calories from fat** =

$$\frac{45 \text{ fat calories}}{121 \text{ total calories}} = \textbf{37\%}$$

Appendix E. Risk Factors for Coronary Artery Disease.

1. Prior heart attack

2. Angina Pectoris (chest pain from heart disease)

3. Male sex

4. Post menopausal female

5. Family history (parent or sibling who had a heart attack or died from sudden death before the age of 55 years)

6. Smoking

7. Hypertension (high blood pressure)

8. Diabetes Mellitus

9. Severe obesity (> 30% overweight)

10. **Elevated Cholesterol Levels**

Appendix F. Calculating the number of calories you need each day.

If your weight has not changed or you have not been dieting, you need approximately 10 calories each day for every pound you weigh to maintain (BMR) your current weight. If you have lost more than 10% of your body weight recently, you will need 7 to 8 calories each day for every pound you weigh. If you have gained more than 10% of your recent body weight, you may need as much as 11 to 12 calories each day for every pound you weigh. In our example we will assume that you have not yet started to lose weight and your current weight is 250 pounds and are 5 feet 10 inches (70 inches) tall. According to appendix B, you are over-weight to obese. Your target weight should be 180 to 190 pounds so you will be in the "good weight" range.

Step 1) You need about 10 calories for every pound you weigh to stay at your current (BMR) weight.

2,500 calories each day = (250 pounds)(10 calories/pound)

Step 2) You are moderately active (chapter two) which means you need an additional 40 percent of your BMR for activity.

1,000 calories for activity = (2,500 calories/BMR)(0.40 BMR)

Step 3) Your total calories needed to maintain your current weight.

BMR	2,500 calories
Activity level	1,000 calories
Total calories	3,500 calories

Step 4) If you want to lose one pound in a week you must eat 500 fewer calories each day (chapter two) than what you need to maintain your current weight.

Total Calories needed to maintain weight	3,500 each day
minus	- 500 calories
Total Calories needed each day to lose one pound in one week	3,000 calories

Glossary

angina (angina pectoris): chest discomfort caused by too little blood flow through the arteries of the heart

apolipoproteins: proteins attached to the different types of cholesterol

atherosclerosis: the buildup of cholesterol and calcium in an artery

cholesterol: a steroid/alcohol eaten or made by the liver

> **total cholesterol (TC):** all the different types of cholesterol added together
>
> **high-density lipoprotein cholesterol (HDL):** carries cholesterol to the liver, commonly referred to as "good cholesterol"
>
> **low-density lipoprotein cholesterol (LDL):** the major source of cholesterol in the blood, commonly referred to as "bad cholesterol"
>
> **intermediate density lipoprotein cholesterol (IDL):** a short lived form of cholesterol except in a small percentage of people
>
> **very-low density lipoprotein cholesterol (VLDL):** primarily triglycerides/fat

calorie: an amount of energy stored in food

carbohydrates: primarily sugars, starches, and fiber

chylomicrons: the primary form of fat once it is eaten and absorbed by our body

epidemiology: the study of the cause of something

fat: fatty acids and glycerol put together—excess calories can be stored in our body as fat. Many types of fat are present in our diet including:

> **hydrogenated fat:** fat that has been stabilized by a man-made process
>
> **monounsaturated fat:** fat which is almost totally saturated
>
> **polyunsaturated fat:** fat which is more flexible including linoleic acid which is needed
>
> **saturated fat:** fat which comes from animals and is solid at room temperature

heart attack: when damage has been done to the heart

HMG Co-A reductase: the enzyme which controls the rate at which cholesterol can be made by the liver

hypercholesterolemia: too much cholesterol

hyperlipidemia: too much cholesterol and/or triglycerides

hypertriglyceridemia: too much triglyceride (fat)

isometric exercise: an exercise where the length of a muscle doesn't change, like weight lifting

isotonic exercise: an exercise where the length of a muscle changes, but no change in tension occurs, like running, walking, bicycling, et cetera.

lipids: primarily fats (triglyceride) and cholesterol

lipoprotein lipase (LPL): an enzyme used to breakdown triglycerides

How to Bypass Your Bypass

lipoprotein: lipids and proteins combined

Positron Emission Tomography (PET): a non-invasive method for determining if you have disease in the arteries of your heart. The most accurate method for determining this.

protein: amino acids, not meat

triglycerides: fats

.